Rachel Webb

Addict's Language
and
A Life of Dubious Virtue

I Dedicate this Book to Joanne

Without her honesty, it would not exist

Addict's Language
(and 'A Life of Dubious Virtue')
'The Addict's Bible'

by
Georgina Wakefield
(and Craig O'Halloran)

APS Publishing
The Old School, Tollard Royal, Salisbury, Wiltshire, SP5 5PW
www.apspublishing.co.uk

British Library Cataloguing in Publication Data
A catalogue record for this book is available from the British Library

© APS Publishing 2004
ISBN 1 9038772 5 3

All rights reserved. No part of this publication may be reproduced, stored in a retrieval system, or transmitted in any form or by any means, electronic, mechanical, photocopying, recording, or otherwise without prior permission from the publisher.
Printed in the United Kingdom by HSW Print, Clydach Vale, Rhondda

Contents

Chapter		Page
	Preface	vii
	Poem: Addict's Language and Introduction	ix
1	The Nursery Rhyme Club	1
2	Dangerous Games	13
3	Six True Case Histories	21
	Preface 2	xcvii
4	Diary: A Life of Dubious Virtue	99
5	N A Meeting	155
6	The Case of Penelope Pittstop	165
7	A Final Summing up and Some Useful Information	175

Preface

Is there a link between schizophrenia and drug addiction? The arguments, research, debates and analysis will continue for a long time yet. I can link them together, not by diagnostics but by chance. Emma decided to visit her old school friend last summer. She was aware that he had been suffering from schizophrenia, and felt guilty for not being supportive. Inadvertently, that pang of guilt generated the production of this book.

The two old friends struck up a relationship from that first visit. His mother was delighted because he had at long last found a friend that really cared. It became apparent, almost from inception that a bond was forming. They spent every spare moment together, thoroughly enjoying each other's company.

My friend started to think 'New Hat' and maybe apple blossom time. It was then I knew I had to tell her the truth. "Yes I agree, my daughter is a lovely, compassionate girl, and yes they do make a lovely couple, but there is something she is that you are not aware of. She is also a drug addict".

The revelation was a bombshell. I had shattered her illusion. After all the painful years of watching her son's loneliness evaporate in the presence of this beautiful girl, this was not something she wanted to hear.

After several, lengthy, tearful discussions, as disbelief abated, we spoke of my world. The world of a parent, whose child had taken that now, well publicised route, one that I had concealed from almost everyone that knew me, probably in an effort to conceal the repugnant fact from myself if the truth be told.

Georgie has encapsulated my feelings in her book and I thank her. I hope all who read her book gain solace. My daughter sent this recently. I smiled for the first time in two years. It read:

Addicts language

> O Lord, I ain't what I ought to be
> *And I ain't what I want to be*
> And I ain't what I'm going to be
> But O Lord, I thank you
> That I ain't what I used to be.

This preface is my proven link between Schizophrenia and Drug Addiction.

Introduction

Scrambled thoughts, washed out feelings, mixed up, screwed up brain
Lives in tatters, numbed emotions, fighting to stay sane
Trunks and trunks of memories, piles of unpaid bills
Parking tickets, speeding fines, used syringes, pills
Filled up ashtrays, empty beer cans, littered crack house floors
Photos screwed up in the hallway, a child she once adored
Go to night school, learn the jargon, addicts foreign tongue
Eats you up, then spits you out with nowhere left to run
Stolen personalities, prisoners in a cell
Shackled firmly no escaping, robots to drugs' hell
Oblivion replaces freedom, then swamps the searing pain
Pathetic losers on the treadmill
'Drugs are so insane'

A bleak outlook

This book is about one of the major problems in society today—drugs. Do you wonder as I do what it will be like in ten, 20 or 30 years time? It's a terrifying prospect. More to the point, what can we do about it? Very little. It's a **bleak outlook**.

One thing is certain, it can only get worse. It's a known fact that users are getting younger and younger and are increasing in numbers all the time. When compiling the research for this book, I talked to many addicts and their families and friends. I have attended Narcotics Anonymous (NA) meetings and watched many bare their souls. These people accepted me being there because they knew that I was writing this book. If you're wondering why, at 55 years of age, I decided to write it—read on. I have learned a lot and have been both shocked and saddened by their stories. Of course, it will take more than a few nursery rhymes and a handful of true life histories to make even a slight dent in this massive problem; nevertheless, it is a comfort to know that I have contributed, if only a little, to something that is so very important. 'Addicts Language' is my protest at the evil I have seen drugs inflict on the lives of so many.

Finding a thread

So, how do I start to find the words? This is what I thought at first; I must try to find a thread among the shattered lives, a beginning. I was at least half way through this book when I realised that I hadn't written the beginning. This is because I always write first the parts that I enjoy the most. So, on May thirtieth at 7am after seven months of writing, I found the thread. I would start with my reasons for writing it.

I've written six books and this is the second one to be published. The first entitled Schizophrenia, a Mother's Story" is the true account of how my younger son developed this harrowing condition at the age of 16 years (he is now 29). Call it bad timing if you like, but I had already started to write a follow up to 'Schizophrenia: A mother's story 'called 'Schizophrenia: Through the maze and fighting back' when some strange things happened that inspired me to write this first. There is growing evidence that smoking cannabis can trigger schizophrenia in <u>certain individuals</u>. I have underlined 'certain individuals' because I do not believe that smoking cannabis causes schizophrenia. I do however believe that it can be the trigger to an underlying pre-disposition. With this in mind I feel that, as we have no way of knowing who those individuals are, it's my duty to write this book.

Only last week a professor of psychiatry was being interviewed on the radio and he said that we can expect a huge rise in the number of people who will develop mental health difficulties in the next few years—so let's look at the facts and the risks.

The facts and the risks

We all know the risks of drug-taking in general, but I would like at this point to highlight the risks, specifically connected to mental health.

Cannabis:	There is more and more evidence that it can trigger schizophrenia in certain individuals.
Ecstasy:	Research shows it can dramatically affect the brain chemistry in animals.
LSD:	Can complicate mental symptoms
Magic Mushrooms:	Can complicate mental symptoms
Amphetamines (Speed):	Can lead to mental illness such as psychosis.

From experience I know that to lose your mind is an extremely hard thing to cope with. I suffered from manic depression for the best part of my adult life and as you know I have had to witness my son's suffering with schizophrenia. Due to these painful experiences and the evidence I have listed above, I see great need for this book.

If only

Let's take cannabis as an example. The cannabis on offer these days—or 'skunk' as they call it—is a far stronger plant than it was when we were young. I speak to many carers who are, like me, very concerned. They have seen young men staring into oblivion. Research will of course continue, but the proof is the amount of young people with a dual diagnosis. Our mental health services are stretched to the limit and it's terrifying to think that this situation will be far worse as time goes on, and this is only about cannabis. It makes you wonder what is in some of the other drugs. If you have youngsters, don't bury your heads in the sand. This is reality, this is happening. Try to educate them, read them one of the case histories, or all of them if need be. Don't end up saying 'if only'.

Addicts language

The following article was featured in 'Your Voice' the quarterly magazine published by 'Rethink', our biggest mental health charity. I've been a member for some years—they do some wonderful work. I rang to ask Terry Hammond (membership manager), who wrote it, for permission to include 'Sleep Walking With Cannabis' and he kindly agreed. We echo the sentiments of many others.

Sleep walking with cannabis

Every day young lives are being wrecked by Cannabis. The desperate and frantic concerns of thousands of parents up and down the country are going unnoticed.

Society seems to be sleep walking into accepting and tolerating this highly dangerous drug. It is time for society to wake up to the fact that by tolerating Cannabis it is risking the mental health of our children and leaving a dreadful legacy for future generations to sort out.

The use of Cannabis has dramatically increased over the last 20 years, particularly amongst young people. Cannabis is now the most popular illicit drug in the western world, with over 60 per cent of school children having tried it; 7 per cent are daily users by the time they are 20. Cannabis is the first illegal drug for 77 per cent of users, compared to crack 1 per cent and ecstasy 4 per cent. There are calls from MPs, journalists, lawyers, people from all walks of life for a more tolerant attitude towards Cannabis. Yet the fears and cries of desperately worried families continue to go unheard and unnoticed. Those who have worked in mental health have known for years that Cannabis can have disastrous effects on some individuals. The anecdotal evidence is screaming at us. Even in our own close circle of friends there are two families who are at their wit's end trying to cope with their sons, both hooked on Cannabis, both totally disengaged with life. Three years ago my own son collapsed at a disco after bingeing all night on Cannabis. When he woke up he had voices in his head; he still has them today. The family is still trying to pick up the pieces.

The anecdotal evidence is now being backed up by hard research; last year the British Medical Journal reported on research in Australia, which linked Cannabis with mental health problems. It showed that early use of Cannabis can lead to depression in later life, especially among woman. Cannabis can provoke anxiety and paranoia. Frequent and high use of cannabis can be a trigger for psychotic episodes.

The key message from the many studies around the globe is that Cannabis can be highly dangerous to both those with a predisposition to mental illness and to those being treated for it. But still society sleepwalks in to tolerating it. One of the main problems, in our view, is the lack of knowledge. Society has yet to wake up to the fact that today's Cannabis is up to 30 times more powerful than the Cannabis used in the 60's. In a survey don by the Guardian last year, 98 per cent believed that Cannabis was safe. This is an appalling indictment on the government's health education policy. To downgrade Cannabis to a class C drug without warning the public of its inherent dangers is, in our view, tantamount to gross negligence. In Holland where Cannabis is more freely used, fewer children actually take it than in the UK.

Why?

Because the Dutch Government has drug education aimed at children focusing on the dangers of Cannabis. Young people in Holland are being given an informed choice, unlike young people in this country.

Our Government appears to be preoccupied with the legal issues of Cannabis instead of informing and promoting the dangers of it. By down grading Cannabis, the Government sent a message to millions of young people that Cannabis is OK. This was

> Parents, CHRISTINE HAMMOND co-ordinator of the Southampton group and TERRY HAMMOND Head of Membership, are still trying to pick up the pieces three years after their son collapsed at a disco after 'bingeing' on cannabis. Here they issue a wake up call.

not the Government's intention but that was the result. Whilst decriminalisation may or may not be a good idea, the central question is surely whether the drug is safe. The answer to this is clearly no.

It is essential therefore that the Government take control of this whole debate. They must warn young people of the inherent dangers of Cannabis. They must tell them that taking Cannabis is playing Russian roulette with their mental health. Failure to do so will result in more lives being wrecked and more families living in despair.

Reproduced by kind permission of Terry Hammond, Membership Manager, 'Rethink'

Sanity roulette

I call it sanity roulette to gamble with your own mind; it is an extremely dangerous game, and no matter which way you look at it, young people are doing this—playing this game. So I think that the reason it took me so long to find the thread for the beginning of this book is that I was torn between my son, who vehemently rejects the idea that smoking cannabis could do so much damage to both his life and ours (and anyone who has read the first book will understand why), and the millions out there who are blissfully unaware that, by lighting a joint, they are taking such an enormous risk.

Looking back I truly believe that my son's illness was already surfacing before he started to smoke cannabis and like many others he started to smoke it to try to help with the dreadful symptoms that this condition inflicts on sufferers. When Chris was 15 years old, I had a phone call from his history teacher who was noticing many changes (as we were) in his behaviour. The onset of schizophrenia is very insidious, almost cunning, the way that it creeps up on you until it finally erupts like a volcano, as it did in my son's case some 18 months later and, yet another warning... smoking cannabis will only make matters worse. On our 14-year journey I have met too many other parents who have sons or daughters with schizophrenia who have quietly asked me "did your son smoke cannabis?" When I have replied "yes" they have said "ours too". So for my own reasons and of course for the families and addicts I've met whose lives have been totally ruined by drugs, I feel that there is a great need for this book and many others on this subject.

None so blind

I wrote this and sent it to seven newspapers; many carers worry as I do about the unsuspecting youngsters and their families who could be about to embark on the same journey as the one we have been on for the past 14 years. As we are totally unaware of who might be predisposed to schizophrenia, surely it's wise to try to deter young people from smoking cannabis. This is why I have called it 'none so blind'. Needless-to-say, none of the newspapers even replied to my poem or the long letter that I sent with it and it did not get printed.

None so blind

Twenty-ninth of January, two thousand and four
Cannabis downgraded, it cuts to the core
There you go kids from b down to c
Now start waving goodbye to your sanity
What gives them the right to make mindless choices
Ignoring so many frantic voices
Mothers who feel so aware of this truth
Who have witnessed this drug rob their young of their youth
Systematically hospitalised
Sons and daughters they no longer recognise
We were there politicians when they were psychotic
With glazed over eyes and movements robotic
We've witnessed the utter devastation
Held their hands through the isolation
Yet you still blunder on with your mindless decision
Ignoring the evidence from those with the vision
We see our services stretched to capacity
Still you don't hear us still you can't see
Visit one acute ward see each tear stained face
Then imagine that's your child stuck in that place
If this tragedy happened to our own Mr Blair
Would it make every one of you far more aware
Statistics don't lie you have to agree
But there's none so blind as the one who can't see

Introduction

Education in schools

A friend of mine—a true professional in mental health— sometimes teaches in schools to try to promote understanding. Recently she was talking to a class of 15-year-olds; she stood in front of the blackboard and asked them to call out all of the names that they associate with schizophrenia. The results were words like:

- Psycho
- Schizo
- Nutter
- Screwball
- Sicko
- Loony

She ended up with nine names and then said, "OK kids, now shout out names that you associate with cancer." Hushed silence with a gasp here and there.

"Come on kids you must be able to think of one surely." Deathly silence. She then said, "Well they are both illness's", and went on to explain how they were in more danger from their next door neighbour than they were from people with schizophrenia; how people with this condition are far more likely to harm themselves and how most violent crimes and murders are committed by people who have never suffered from a mental illness. She said that these young people were really shocked that they had it all so wrong.

Labels are not the answer, whether these are for a mental illness or dual diagnosis. What is needed is more and more education in schools so that ignorance doesn't have the opportunity to become entrenched.

Labels

Recently I have been asked to use part of this book for training staff who are working with dual diagnosis clients.

The trust in question were receiving far too many complaints about staff having bad attitudes. When you're a law abiding person, it must often be really difficult to keep a lid on your feelings, especially when you see the lengths that some of these people will go to in order to feed their addiction. I asked Tony Marsh once what helped him to finally get clean following ten failed attempts. He said, "I met a support worker who actually treated me like a human being." I am not suggesting that this would work for others—who knows? But at least it worked for him; I do hate the term dual diagnosis; two labels instead of one.

Labels—Double d or dual diagnosis

Double D or dual diagnosis
Addictions drugs, full blown psychosis
Double whammy double D
A game called' labels' play with me
Lets all play a game called labels
Which label would you prefer?
I've got a good un— it's schizo
She's got two though, ask her
Well I've got loony and scag head
I've got more—there's smack head too
Let's try labelling other illnesses
Like diabetes—cancer too
Nothing springs to your mind?
How about tumour face?
Say that in the street and they'll lynch you mate
That really is a disgrace
But what's the problem, it's still an illness
Just like all of the rest?
Yeah, but with cancer there's compassion and sympathy
You're treated real good and that's best
But we all know that both are an illness
How come one has a label
That's easy people don't understand
They see us as evil, unstable
That's just how it is mate

Introduction

Things won't change you take it from me
But with a label like dual diagnosis
It's a double whammy, double D

Giving it a Try

One of the lessons I have learned through my son's illness is that we don't really know about anything unless it touches our own lives. I've come to realise that although I get frustrated by the ignorance and stigma that attaches itself to mental illness, I too would have probably thought that most people with schizophrenia are axe wielding maniacs; I would have been taken in by the sensational stories that the papers provide simply to sell more papers, when in actual fact 98% of sufferers are the gentlest, kindest souls on this earth. And statistically you are in more danger from your next-door neighbour.

Although I brought up two sons, I knew very little about drug addiction. This wasn't happening in my life so why should I concern myself with it? Then out of the blue one day, someone handed me an old battered grey diary which had been named 'A Life Of Dubious Virtue', the following poem entitled 'White Horses', two small birds in a cage (not live), a china cross and a copy of the serenity prayer. The strangest thing of all was as she handed me the copy of the Serenity Prayer, I handed a copy that I'd typed for her. This young woman is one of the case histories in this book and is herself addicted to heroin. I found this all very symbolic—the caged birds being a mirror of her existence and the cross and the prayer I saw as symbolic of God, and he's very prevalent in the 12 steps of recovery taken by NA members... and the diary? Well that's a story on its own.

Riding White Horses
Author unknown

Come ride the white horse the horse dealer cried
You'll have a great trip he casually lied
The first rides for free those words did the trick
I rode off on her back but after felt sick

The next time I saw him I asked of his horse
I wanted to ride he said "but of course"
The horse rocked from heaven to hell with my soul
No longer the master, the horse had control
The dealer looked different, horns, hooves and a tail
Upon my return a guaranteed sale

White horses cost plenty and my money had gone
So I stole for my habit though I knew it was wrong
My body was sick, I quickly grew thin
But inside white horses are not allowed in
Now my horse days are over but the memories don't fade
So if you ride the white horse ride it well
For the white horse of heroin will take you to hell

Chapter 1
The Nursery Rhyme Club

Join now. Free membership to anyone who would like to join. Our slogan is

'Memberships free if you care to join start with a puff and end up in the groin.

Hey Diddle Diddle

Hey diddle diddle, the cat's on the fiddle,
Ran off with the brown-stained spoon.
The cow's got a habit and so has the rabbit,
They're both scared of the big fat baboon

Hey diddle diddle, the end to this riddle,
The gear cost them all of a monkey.
The fat cat laughed to see such fun,
When they each turned into a junkie.

Humpty and Junkie

Humpty and junkie sat on a wall
Humpty and junkie had a great fall
Humpty recovered, yet loved ones and friends
Couldn't put Junkie together again.

Addicts language

Little Miss Muffett

Little Miss Muffett sat on her tuffet rolling a big fat joint
Along came a dealer who sat down beside her, determined to show her the point.
So he gave her a needle to stick in her vein,
He sold her some brand new gear
Miss Muffet's a loser, now she's a user
And from now on she'll pay very dear.

Little Boy Blue

Little boy blue come puff on this pipe
Shoot up in a nice new vein
The sheep's in the crack house the cow's gone in rehab
As he tries to get clean yet again

Little boy blue, come sample some crack
Or come chase the dragon with me
But before you start scoring remember life will be boring
From now on you'll never be free

The Owl and the Pussycat

The owl and the pussycat went to the crack house to buy themselves a new spoon
The fat cat dealer said "Sample my wares and you'll be in another world soon"
The owl and the pussycat scored 'til they dropped, they could no longer feel any pain
Now they lay in the gutter, the pussycat's dead, and the owl is completely insane

Little Jack Horner

Little Jack Horner sat in the corner crying for his wife and kids
He filled up his syringe then prepared a new pipe, his future is clean on the skids
Little Jack Horner is sick of his corner, a prisoner now in a cell

His moods are haphazard, emotions are stunted, and he's lost all sense of smell

Little Jack Horner go back to your corner, don't expect the world to care
Start going to rehab take positive steps
Even though it will be hard to bear.

Little Bo Peep

Little Bo Peep is losing her sleep
She's a fat cat drug dealer's daughter
Her flock are lining up at the gate
She watches them go to the slaughter

Little Bo Peep think of the pain
Don't allow them to go through the gate
If you don't save them from the dealer's gun
They will end up full of blind hate

So Little Bo Peep, dig down real deep
And give them all your guidance
Show them the way to keep drugs at bay
Or they'll drag their young lives far behind them.

The Counting House

The dealer's in the counting house
Counting out his money
The user's in the gutter
His life is not so funny
His girlfriend's in the parlour
Preparing her next hit
Down swoop the drug squad
And tells them "this is it"

Mary, Mary Quite Contrary

Mary, Mary, quite contrary
How does your cannabis grow?
It grows well in the roof space
You can tell which is her place
Coz the roof isn't covered in snow
Mary, Mary quite contrary
Are your moods cannabis-induced?
She's up in the loft
Cutting some down
Shall we watch her go through the roof?

Little Polly Flinders

Little Polly Flinders, sat among the cinders,
Planning her next big hit.
Her mother came and caught her, she scolded her young daughter
Now Polly's deep in the shit.

Little Polly Flinders has found her mother hinders
Her plans for obtaining her drugs,
She sells her body for a fiver then they sidle up beside her,
Losers, dealers and thugs.

Jack and Jill

Jack and Jill went up the hill both looking pasty pale
They were mocked by the rabbit when he heard of their habit
He declared they were destined to fail.
Jack and Jill went back up the hill, they heard the rabbit mutter
"Sad pair of losers, they'll end up in jail. Either there or in the gutter"
Jack said to Jill, "let's start a new life, we will drive that old rabbit to ground"
They both started rehab and came out clean
So they ended up both safe and sound.

Wicked Evil Heroin

Wicked evil heroin
Runs through your veins
Fucks up your future
Then comes the pains
Wicked evil heroin
Robs you of your life
Takes away your job, your home
Your kids and your wife.

Wicked evil heroin
Lurks in your syringe
You think you are in control of it
And then you start to binge
You thought it was cool
You believed you had life sussed
Now your haggard, sad appearance
Fills you with disgust.

Wicked evil heroin, whack some in your groin
Membereship's free to losers; who'd like to join?

Ten Little Skag Heads

Ten little skag heads sitting in a line
One got hooked on cannabis, then there were nine
Nine little skag heads sitting on the gate
One went into rehab, and then there were eight
Eight little skag heads thought they'd gone to heaven
One died from overdose, and then there were seven
Seven little skag heads needing a quick fix
One copped hold of dodgy gear, and then there were six
Six little skag heads fighting to survive
One chased the dragon, and then there were five
Five little skag heads knocked at the dealer's door
He still owed from the last lot then there were four
Four little skag heads longing to be free
One was caught red handed, then there were three

Addicts language

Three little skag heads feeling very blue
Sniffed crack up their nostrils then there were two
Two little skag heads and a battle to be won
One fell down the gutter, then there was one
So if you're that skag head
Then you're some poor bastard's son
Get clean to show the other nine
That battles can be won

Ring A Ring O Roses

Ring-o ring-o-roses a pocket full of cannabis
Give me crack, heroin or speed
Atishoo, atishoo I'm down on my uppers
Fulfilling the fat dealer's greed

Ring-o ring-o roses a pocket full of problems
My habit's reached its fifteenth year
I'm using in the groin now, sad, sorry, daft cow
I shed yet another futile tear.

The Grand Old Fat Cat Dealer

The grand old fat cat dealer
Supplies many druggies on his turf
He marched that rival to the top of the hill
And beat him for all he was worth

Coz when your time is up, it is up
And when his sales are down they are down
And when he sees a drop in his takings
He'll bury you deep in the ground

Yesterday he was up he was up
But today he is wearing a frown
Last thing we'd heard of his rival
He was lying on a slab in a gown.

Climbing Up the Spout

Sad and lonely young boy, climbed up the spout
Down came the cannabis and flushed the young boy out
Out went his life, down cam the pain
Pathetic lonely junkie, going clean insane.

Hardened junkie thug now, climbed up the spout
Down came the drugs squad, flushed the junkie out
Down came his sentence, thrown into jail
Did a five-year sentence, came out looking pale

Evil big cat dealer, climbed up the spout
Down came all the big bucks, cleaned all the skag heads out
Out came all the treasures, for him to enjoy
Which flushed away the memories of a sad a lonely boy

Clever solvent criminal, climbed up the spout
Down came his henchmen, all on the tout
A mansion now in Chigwell, two Jags stand in the drive
Opulence galore coz the criminal survived

Bathing

Skag, dealer and junkie went down to the sea to bathe
The dealer is bathing in splendour
The other two couldn't be saved
The dealer resides in a mansion, two Mercs stand in his drive
He dances on the losers' graves
Coz skag head and junkie both died.

The Devil's Parlour

"Come into the parlour," said the devil once to me
"Enjoy a life without a care, forever young and free"
With no resistance or respect I ventured right on in,
Expecting only pleasures, not depravity and sin.
Once through the door there's no escape
So entangled in his web
I sold my soul, became his slave and found misery instead
He ruled my life, shattered my spirit and stole my liberty
I longed for freedom and craved the care
My loved ones gave to me.
But I'd sampled of his evil wares, I'd tried heroin and speed
I became a stranger to myself in my selfish, treacherous greed
So if he invites you in then you decline
Don't argue, save your breath
Slam hard the devil's parlour door
For it's he who plans your death.

Standing In The Dock

Hickory dickory dock
A young man ran up the clock
On the strike of one his nightmares begun
Hickory dickory dock

Hickory dickory dock
He has no idea when to stop
On the strike of three, he was no longer free
Hickory dickory dock

Hickory dickory dock
The junkie ran up the clock
Now the clock has struck five, his life's hard to survive
Hickory dickory dock

Hickory dickory dock
The skag head scored 'til he dropped
When the clock struck nine, t'was the end of the line
Hickory dickory dock

Hickory dickory dock
Tell me what you've learned from this shock
If you're tempted to score, ask yourself "Christ what for?"
Hickory dickory dock.

One Two, Sniff Some Glue

1-2 sniff some glue
3-4 start to score
5-6 drugs are sick
7-8 this life I hate
9-10 rehab again
11-12 why did I delve?
13-14 what do drugs mean
15-16 an end to your dream
17-18 end up hating
19-20 life's so empty
So 1-2 what do I do?
3-4 never score

See Saw

See saw give us a draw
Then Johnnie's life's a disaster
Coz it will take every penny he earns
And drugs will become his master

Mary Had A Little Sniff

Mary had a little sniff she drew some up her nose
It blew away her septum but that's the way it goes
Now she awaits her operation she winces at the pain
To help her cope she does some dope
And sniffs some more cocaine.

Little Tommy Tucker

Little Tommy Tucker is a naughty little f*****
What shall we sell him to make our bread and butter?
We'll give young Tommy heroin
We'll give him crack and speed
Tommy's such a silly boy
He's supplied our every need.

Diddle Diddle Heroin

Diddle diddle heroin my son Jack
He got into speed and he got into crack
One young life ruined no way back
Diddle diddle heroin my son Jack.

Tom, Tom, The Junkie's Son

Tom Tom the junkie's son
Stole some gear then away he run
The gear was crap Tom took the rap
Tom fell into the dealer's trap

Pat-A-Cake, Pat-A-Cake Dealer Man

Pat-a-cake, pat-a-cake, dealer man
Supply me with gear as fast as you can
Split it and cut it and mark it with D [for dunce]
Make sure there's enough for my mates and me

The Crooked Dealer

There was a crooked dealer who walked a crooked mile
He found a naïve young man and took away his smile
He introduced him to some skag heads, they all formed a ring
The young man blew their cover when they all began to sing
Now he sits in prison his only friends a mouse
The dealer made it big time, you should see his house.

Simple Simon

Simple Simon met a dealer going to the fair
Said Simple Simon to the dealer
Let me try your wares
Said the dealer to Simple Simon
Show me first your dough
Then I'll show you my lovely rocks
Poor Simon was so slow
Said Simple Simon to the dealer
Sir I have no money
So he cut his throat from ear to ear
And found it very funny

Singa Songa Cannabis

Sing a songa cannabis pocket full of crack
Down came the dealer shot his rival in the back
Coz when the dealer's angry his rival's full of fear
Wasn't he a silly boy to owe him for his gear.

Addicts language

Junkie Boys Picnic

If you go to see your dealer today you're in for a big surprise
If you dare to sample his gear today
You'll hardly believe your eyes
For every junkie that ever there was
Was gathered there for certain because
Today is the day we laugh at what drugs stand for,

If you go down to the crack house today
You're in for your biggest hit
If you dare to sample his wares today
You'll end up in deep shit
So heed my words "don't be tempted to score"
You're in danger of becoming a skag head bore
Coz today's the day we laugh at what drugs stand for

Picnic time for junkie boys
All those junkie boys are having a very bad time today
See them crying out for more
As we watch their young lives ebb away

Picnic time for junkie boys
All the junkie boys are trying hard to find a vein
Watch them struggle more and more
It's the only way to ease their pain

So if you go down to the crack house today
You're really in for a laugh
The junkie boys are crying today
So try not to follow their path
Coz every junkie that sampled a joint
Has ended up wondering "what was the point?"
Coz today's the day we all laugh at what drugs stand for.

Chapter 2

Dangerous Games

Join our club but abide by the rules, there's no room for losers, junkies or fools
We share board games, membership's free. Join and we'll own your sanity.

Our two slogans are contradicting each other like the book title, '*A Life Of Dubious Virtue*'

Join Our Youth Club
For 12 – 16 year olds
We share board games
Membership's FREE
Don't join if you want your sanity

Blind Man's Bluff

Three blind kids, three blind kids
See how they score, see how they score
They think they're cool and they think it's a laugh
None of them knows what's at the end of the path
Their mums are crying, their dad's filled with wrath
  Over three blind kids

Three blind kids, three blind kids
See what they use, see what they use
Pipes and burners and crack cocaine
The next step will be H to dull their pain
But it's nothing ventured and nothing gained
  With three blind kids

Three blind kids, three blind kids
Two don't exist, two don't exist
They owed the dealer for stacks of gear
His throat was cut from ear to ear
His mate OD'd or so I hear
  Three blind kids

One blind kid, one blind kid
Finally saw the light, restored was his sight
He went into rehab and came out clean
They say he's still haunted by terrible dreams
Don't follow their path if you see what I mean
  Poor blind kids

Modern games

'Dangerous Games' has been written from an older age group's point of view, starting with 'Solvent King' which is two little boys having a conversation at school about glue sniffing. This is the first one that I wrote and is similar to 'The Nursery Rhyme Club', paving the way for others, such as 'Five Stones', which suggests that the games children play these days are very different from the games which we played in the 50s. Hopefully, it will make people think and highlight how, if we don't make these comparisons and show our own kids, where it could all end up?

Solvent King

Have a sniff, d'ya wanna whiff?
I love going high
I use the dosh mum gives for nosh
To fly up to the sky
Don't believe ya s'only glue
My dad's got some indoors
He uses it for loads of fings
Even tiles on my mums' floors
Take a sniff wanna whiff?
S'better than play station
Don't cost much I fink it's cool
Such a great sensation
Gis some more 'ere then – let me try it
Christ it's great where d'ya buy it?
I nicked that from the corner shop
I've got some butane too
I've tried the lot 'I'm solvent king'
My favourite is glue
My bruvver started yonks ago
But now e's into spliffs
He loved sniffin' just like us
G'is another whiff.

Jigsaw Puzzles

Imagine a giant jigsaw
Each piece represents a life
A mother, father, a daughter, a son
A husband and a wife
You try hard but it won't fit together
The pieces too big or too small
It causes you pain and frustration
Your back's up against the wall
The reason it won't fit together
Is one of them got into drugs
Out of the window went self respect
Along with the laughs and the hugs
The misshapen pieces reflect their lives
And though they've tried many times in vain
Short of a miracle the pieces are worthless
And will not fit together again.

The Devil's Fire

Dangerous games ain't worth playing
Avoid them and life remains sweet
Never
Give in to temptation – drugs are
Evil beyond belief
Remember the lives that they've shattered
Or the ones that have even been lost
Understand the life you've been living be
Sensible and see the high cost

Give in and you'll enter
A nightmare you'll slowly sink into the
Mire, escape from the
Evil that they're
Sure to inflict and keep away from
    The devil's fire

Dangerous Games

Sanity Roulette

*Roll up, roll up for sanity roulette
The rules are clear and straight
Your opponent offers some choices
A wrap, some crack, or H*

*Roll up, roll up for sanity roulette
He'll convince you you're playing well
If he gets out the wheel for a game
The first throw could take you to hell
The dealer holds the ace card
He's rich, he's evil and he's hard*

*In a game called sanity roulette
Your minds in the frame for this bet
For a false fix don't gamble your mind
Madness can be so unkind
So decline the wrap and hedge your bet
Don't lose your mind playing sanity roulette.*

Scrabble

*Scramble your thoughts scramble your brain
Collect your meagre prize
Remember a life that you used to have
Before this bleak disguise*

*Live your life, enjoy loved one's hugs
Scrabble is safer than any drugs
Future is brighter for everyone,
so always remember, Drugs ain't fun*

Play safe, ignore the rabble, play a game of scrabble.

Draughts

The dealer chooses black
While you will plump for white
His draughts soon make a stack
While you're a sorry sight

He counts up his latest hoard
As he takes you right across the board
So in theory who got the last laugh?
In the dealer's game of draughts

Three Card Brag

Three card brag a game of cards
To lose would be a choker
"He who deals, wins" that's what they say
But look who got the joker

Shuffle them well and deal the pack
Avoid the nickname skag
Make your move and play the Jack
Win this time in three card brag

Ladders and Snakes

Up the ladders and down the snakes
One small puff is all it takes
Value your life see through the fakes
Steer away from ladders and snakes

Dangerous Games

Monopoly

The dealer has the monopoly
Her rarely goes to jail
His opponent doesn't fair so well
In fact he's set to fail

As they travel round and round the board
The dealer plans each move
Each throw of the dice works well for him
He knows each niche, each groove

Your score is low, a penalty
The dealer wins once more
He buys a mansion in Hyde Park
With opulence galore

So before you play, think long and hard
Then hopefully you'll see
The odds are stacked against you now
It's dealer's monopoly.

5 Stones

D'ya wanna play druggies, dealers and cops
Na let's take the bus and go look round the shops.
Shoppin's real boring I say we play
Bags I'm the dealer whaddya say?
You can be druggie coz you look the part
Are you two ready, time to start?
I'll be cop then, I'll do the raid
I like playin' dealer coz he's highest paid
We can use mum's brown sugar coz it looks like gear
Let's bag it up first, give us some 'ere
 'As it been cut or is it real pure
Best we ask dealer coz I ain't sure
Bang, bang, bang, dealer's got a gun
Shot the cop's kneecaps just for fun
I'm always the copper I 'ate this game

Yella-belly, that's your name
Yella should 'ave been born yonks ago
My dad reckons life was betta tho'
My dad and ees mate played 5 stones
On the pavement if ya pleez
My dad says he loved playin' 5 stones
They'd play it down on their knees
Where's yella-belly, I fink 'es gone 'ome
Probably gone ta play 5 stones.

Happy Families

"The family's hooked", laughs the dealer
Mum, dad, son and daughter
Rubs his hands together, good for business
Four lambs to the slaughter

They spend a fortune, always knocking
He laughs once more with glee
"I think it's great, they're so together"
Such a happy family.

Chapter 3
Case Histories

The Feeling Wheel

(used in rehab)

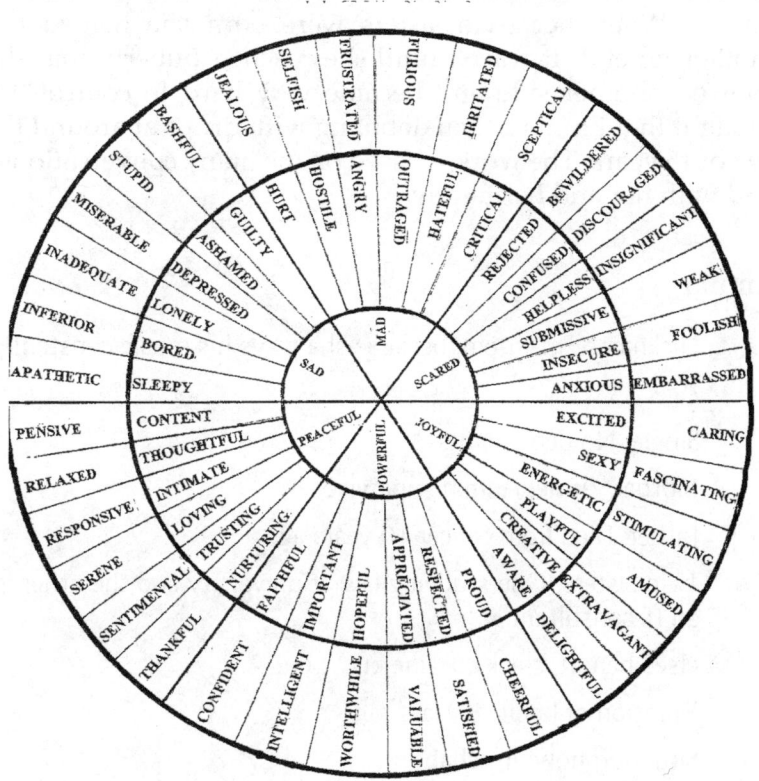

Only one of these case histories has given permission for his real name to be used — Tony Marsh. In all the other cases, their names have been changed at their own or their families request.

I've tried to vary the case histories and explain in as much detail as possible the effects on both their lives and their families. The first and last case histories are the longest due to the length of time I spent with the people involved.

As you will see, the first one I did spend a lot of time with. This young woman was not abused or neglected as a child. Her mother told me that although she was a charming child, she also had an extremely stubborn and determined nature. When her twin sisters were born she helped her mother no end. It wasn't until she reached puberty that she showed another side and became very hard to control. It's thought that Emma began dabbling with drugs at around the age of 15 years. The work is based on the many conversations I had with her and her family.

Emma

Nickname Em-in-em, because she plays his music constantly

Age: 33

Single; No dependants

Mother: Anne, Admin Supervisor

Father: Died from cancer 10 years ago

Twin sisters: One studying law at university and the other is an IT consultant

Uses heroin, crack cocaine etc… etc…

Duration of habit: 8 years

Situation now: In rehab

Hopes for the future: to stay clean

Physical description: height 5'2" her weight fluctuates from between 7 and 8 stone.

Considering how long she's been using and how much gear she's been into, Em's appearance is good most of the time. Long blond hair, dark at the roots, good figure and legs. Pretty face and blue/green eyes, dresses very extrovertly, ad-fab style. Em has 30 pairs of designer sunglasses and she likes wearing headgear. When she's in control she looks exceptionally good, when she's not she looks entirely different.

Emma's partner in crime, or her co-dependant as she calls him, is case history No 2 (Chaz: Nickname, 'The Hawk'). Her story starts with how they spend their days, bearing in mind that so far she has never had to sell herself—Chaz wouldn't hear of it and she can't bear to think about it, so Chaz has the responsibility of providing enough cash through shoplifting and burglary to support both their habits.

I wrote 'Life's a Dream' following a conversation with Emma. She talked about her life before drugs and how she often cried when she thought about how different her life would have been had she not become an addict. Emma and Chaz did not even talk much to each other; if they did, it was always about how they'd get enough for the next hit. She said that they would take it in turns to go first. I really tried hard to understand, but it is like everything in life, you have to experience things before you can really understand them. She promised me that she would always let me know how she was. I didn't hear from her for weeks; I left many messages on her mobile, which was always on answer phone. When we finally saw each other she said that she didn't have any money to put credits on her phone. She looked dreadful, much thinner and had pick marks all over her arms and face. She didn't seem to care what might happen to her. As for her family, no matter how many times I tried to reason with her and explain that they had come to the end of the line, she had no conception whatsoever of what it was like for them to watch her ruining her life. She just thought that they were selfish bastards; she seemed unable to see herself for what she was—a junkie. It became clearer all the time that the only thing that really mattered to Em was where the next hit was coming from.

Life is a Dream

The Hawk does all the thieving, she drives the getaway car
Sometimes close to the crack house, sometimes they travel quite far
They contact their usual dealer on a well worn mobile phone
They appear very much together, in reality they're alone.
Conversations are thin on the ground apart from "pass me my gear"
It glistens and drops from her chin, yet another futile tear.
She dreams of the life she once had and the friends she had from school
She really thought she was clever, convinced herself she was cool.
She catches sight of herself in the window
Her dark haunted eyes stare right back
She's repulsed by her wretched appearance
But her emotions are stretched on a rack
So it's back to chasing the dragon; sordid, tragic, obscene
Two more punctured, well worn veins then oblivion
Peace "Life's a dream"

Freedom

I wrote Freedom after going with Em to her flat in London. She had never actually got round to moving in and this was the fourth time her family had helped her to get her own home, move her in, furnish it and clear any outstanding debts. In the kitchen was a brand new fridge freezer with some rotting meat in it, a brand new washing machine that had never been plumbed in, an antique leather armchair, and a mattress on the floor. The place was strewn with belongings, there were three trunks full of possessions. Em told me that she had trunks in the previous three flats and that she must phone the new tenants to arrange to pick them up but, even as she was saying it, I knew that it would never happen. There were also piles of unopened letters, mostly bills and parking fines. I mentioned how warm it was and she laughed as she felt one of the three radiators that she had left on some three months ago, the last time she went to the flat was with Chaz to score. One of Em's sisters told me that she had already been to the flat to clean it up, she had removed 16 carrier bags filled with syringes and twisted baco-foil and brown stained spoons. She had also cleaned the flat as best she could. Following one of their many arguments, she told Em that she no longer wanted anything to do with her. A few weeks later she had seen Em in the street and hadn't recognised her at first. She was filthy, her hair hung in grease and there was snot smeared across her face; although she was both sad and disgusted, she gave her money and held her for a while. Although the twins are both opposed to drug addiction, they are still very supportive of their big sister and travel miles to visit her at the weekend despite working hard all week. They both help her as much as they can and they love her very much despite her addiction.

Readers must bear in mind that I wrote Freedom when Em was making a conscious effort to get clean. Her obsession with belongings was similar to Mr Trebus who was in the BBC series A Life Of Grime; it was as if she was scared to throw things away hence the trunks of belongings

Freedom

She's an extremely Dubious Virtue a maze of contradictions
Haphazard, demanding, destructive
She overflows with inhibitions
Trunk after trunk of possessions disjointed and overflowing
Out if cinque distorted emotions dictate where her life has been going
She's lost within this muddle, buried beneath her treasures
Incarcerated within the caskets robbing her of life's pleasures
Jeans and dresses and trousers stack upon stack upon stack
She struggles to get them on hangers
Rack after rack after rack
Rows of shoes in every colour every pair
Reflecting her greed
Bangles that shimmer and glitter
Not one of them filling her need

She has searched in every corner
She has turned over every stone
Sought oblivion in evil chemicals
Then admitting defeat she came home
Now a whirlwind of tattered emotions furious frantic and fast
No goal, no hope, and no future
She releases her demons at last
She's putting it all in some order
Banishing false fixes she bought
In black plastic bags neatly piled
A mirror of what she's been taught
Possessions Christ who needs them?
Phoney highs are all their good for
Robbing her of her freedom is it lost forever more?

Sweet relief in organisation
How she needs her life to be
Slowly retrieving true pleasures at last
Happy, content, and free
She soars up into life's sunset a beautiful snow white dove
Her thirst now quenched by "Peace of mind"
She's home at last to love

Prefix to 'Reaching the Shore'

I really hoped that if I could get her to see how brave my son had had to be during his 14-year battle with schizophrenia; it might have helped her to be strong. Sometimes the whole thing would make me angry simply as she had an answer, hard as it was she had a way out. I think it is unfair because drug addiction is self-inflicted, what do you believe? Are drugs addicts people with a greed for life, people who are not satisfied with the normal pleasures of life, have they all been born with addictive personalities? Do some become addicts to blot out the pain, pressures of work, morbid curiosity? I believe the answer to these questions is, yes.

I wrote reaching the shore to highlight the similarities between my son's illness and drug addiction in an emotional sense.

The time they spent together, my son and Emma did help each other. She would often say "It's so sad about Chris and it's not his fault that this has happened to him." She was always very honest about herself and did not make any excuses for her addiction. Although their problems were different, they seemed to really understand each other and would often spend hours talking. She came round recently with her mum, we sat in the garden drinking tea. Anne and I were chatting, as were Em and Chris. Later she said that she could see the sadness in Christian's eyes and it reminded her of how sad she felt herself. Two young people both with huge problems and yet I do feel that they will always be there for each other. In the short time that they were together she did her best to be a good friend to Christian and I will never forget that, even with her problems she was more of a friend to Chris than anyone else has been in the past. This kindness must run in the family as her twin sisters have also included him in their lives, and they have all tried really hard to help me with this book. Reaching the shore is about their equally hard plights.

Reaching the shore

Both addicted to drugs, drugs of a different kind
Hers to blot out the pain, his to control his mind
Both searching for the answers, answers they just cant find
He needs to take things slowly; she needs to search her mind
Both disillusioned by living
They search for the answers in vain
Hers a fight for survival his a fight to stay sane
They're battered by life's pressures
As they fight each relentless storm
Their boat of life so fragile
Alienated from the norm
She battles to fight her addictions he fights the demons within
Casualties of life's hardships this waste of life's pleasure a sin
Both addicted to pain, pain of a different kind

Addicts language

Hers in lost emotions, his within his mind
Both desperate for a normal life in many diverse ways
Dragged down by separate journeys, bogged down by the days
Yet the answers are there they must find them
If it takes forever more
Will they master each search for contentment?
Will their boat of life reach the shore?

When Em started yet again to try to get clean she said something to me that led me to write the next poem entitled "Addicted to Addicts"

We were driving along and she started to laugh. "Do you know something Georgie?" she said "I'm not addicted to drugs any more, I'm addicted to addicts" She then went on to tell me that she had pledged to attend some 90 AA meetings in as short a time as she could cope with, and she did try. Sometimes I would phone her on her mobile and she would say, "I can't talk, I'm in another meeting"

Addicted to Addicts

We're all addicted to addicts swapped for our own drug addictions
Strength in so many numbers, all sharing the same afflictions
Obsessed with getting clean, engulfed by all of our meetings
We plan each one meticulously, our pain providing our teachings
Who's been clean twenty years? How many have finally reached ten?
We bathe in the glory of others, comforted yet again
Hands up those who've just started, many hands go up in the air
We strip ourselves reveal our crimes, our painful shame is laid bare
Ninety meetings in 90 days from one venue to another
Each with their own horror story as we struggle to recover
Tenacious to our cause, an army of lost souls
With our precious stories of life before drugs, united in our goals

Addictive personalities, a way of life, a culture
He waits in the wings for the pickings
Temptation the devil's vulture
But there's comfort in our addiction
Determination will never waver
Although we're addicted to addicts
This addiction could be our saviour

Responsibilities

The following work stems from the many conversations I shared with Emma's family. Some are based on my thoughts, others are based on theirs. The family, like my own, have been through every emotion in the book. Anne has lost count of the times she's disowned her daughter, but never for very long. Recently she told me she had decided to go away for a week with friends. On her way home from work, the day before she went away, she stopped to pick up a few last minute things from the shops. When she got back to the car for no apparent reason she began to cry and couldn't stop. This tends to happen more and more lately she told me; again, it's so similar to my situation. You never get used to the pain, if anything, the longer it goes on, the harder it gets, like being on an emotional roller coaster ride that never stops. The whole family share the same journey. Her twin sisters, who are no bother at all, dread ringing their mother. As one of them explained, "all she goes on about is Em and her addiction and I'm sick to death of hearing about it. We've all tried to help her time after time but she throws it in our faces. What about our lives? Don't we count? Although we feel sorry for mum, we can only take and do so much. I sometimes think Em likes the life she's living and with all the will in the world and the desire to get clean is down to her, but she's very good at shirking her responsibilities." As all addicts are.

Based on a conversation with me and Em's twin sisters.

Getting You Clean

We loved to play together
Your future looked so bright
Now we can't bear to look at you
You're such a sorry sight
Your clothes aren't clean or ironed
Your hair is such a mess
Your teeth were always white and clean
And what's that down your dress?
You need a damned good shower
There's snot around your nose
Your arrogance disgusts us both
"That's just the way life goes"
How we loved to play together
Life was but a dream
Big sister you disgust us both
But how can we get you clean?

Wicked Evil Stuff
[Anne to Emma]

Did I not give her everything?
My heart, my life, my soul
We'd talk about her future
And what would be her goal
A good career, good husband, kids
A home, a big flash car
Oblivious to the evil
Drugs have dragged her down so far
Was she pushed out when the twins were born?
She craved so much attention
I never dreamed she'd sample drugs
I should have thought to mention
I've let her down, that's obvious
My love was not enough
Yet the answer stares me in the face
                        Wicked evil stuff!!

Making Amends

You thought you could control it
In your usual arrogance, thieving for a living
None of this makes sense
But you thought that you were different
A cut above the rest, four times you've tried to kick it
You say you did your best

You said you'd never sell your body
That filled you with disgust
But your craving for the next big hit means selling it's a must
An existence of depravity yet you laughed at all your friends
It's them that's got the last laugh and it's too late
  to make amends

Emma lost many of her friends through here habit, mainly because she was forever disappearing and none of them knew where she was.

Denial

Totally in denial she can't see the wood for the trees
One glance is all that it takes, drugs have brought her down to her knees
Totally denies all knowledge, convinces herself that she's clean
Her family bury their heads in the sand
They can't cope with another scene
Three times this year she's tried it, each time she said this is it
Bitter disappointment deeper in the s***
So the next time that she makes you a promise
Cross her heart this time it's final
Try to remember these words
She's totally in denial

Breaking my heart is about a conversation I had with Emma's mum recently. She's at her wits end and wonders how much more she can cope with. Her relationship with the twins is very strained and some people have lost patience over the years. Anne is not angry with them, she understands where they are coming from. Some see Anne as weak for not disowning her daughter. I wonder if they stop to think what that really means. Though Anne knows she can't save her daughter from this awful life and although she knows that Emma uses her for her own convenience, and even though every waking moment is filled with anxiety and fear and sadness, Emma is still her child and that will never change nor will the fact she can never stop loving her.

The following work was written after a conversation with Anne; she was trying to explain how hard it is for her at work. Only a few people who she trusts know about her problems and this is to explain how she feels like screaming it out when her colleagues are saying you look tired or your not yourself today. Emma told me herself that as they were always in a hurry when they were out working [shoplifting]; they would take a chance and park the car as near as they could to the shop, due to this they were forever getting parking fines and we are not talking about a few; they amounted to thousands of pounds. If it wasn't parking fines, it was speeding tickets or fines for driving in the bus lane and all the time Anne was working to pay them.

Breaking My Heart

For quickness I slipped on your housecoat
The one that's like a Dalmatian
It scratched my hand twisted Baco-foil
Yet another painful sensation
I unwrapped it and there in the middle
Half a spoonful of brown grain like sand
Even after four years it can shock me
By now I should understand
My imagination runs riot
I see you melting it on your spoon
You shuffle out to the kitchen
How I wish you were back in my womb
I'm torn by so many emotions
I feel bitter and angry and sad

Part of me wants to kick you hard
How have things got this bad?
The foil simply mirrors your addiction
It's cold, it's twisted, it's sharp
I end up with my arms around you
Saying "Emma you're breaking my heart"

Far Away

Work tomorrow I dread the thought
It's such a foreboding feeling
I need to sleep but sleep evades me
I stare hard at the ceiling
My brain stays in the on position
I'm locked in anxiety
I close my eyes but crack house floors
Are all that I can see
Your crumpled body amongst the debris
So plain in my minds eye
A needle sticks out from your ankle
I'm terrified you'll die
My body aches, my brain's exhausted
Yet still it can't close down
My first born child amongst this evil
Round and round and round
I need to sleep – work tomorrow
I toss – I turn – I pray
I close my eyes to try once more
But sleep is far away

Emotionally Bankrupt

Robbed of my money stripped bare of feelings
Emotionally bankrupt that's me
Exhausted, depleted and sick of the struggle
Like you I can never be free
Desperate, desolate and craving for peace
Sick to death of your chequered past
Like you I'm a victim of your drug addiction

With its trail of destruction so vast
 Worn out by the talking – my on going battle
Of trying to make you see
That drugs rule the game and we're always the losers
Emotionally bankrupt that's me

My thoughts on Emma

Caught Within The Headlights

Beta blockers, tranquillisers, amphetamines or speed
Uppers, downers, lost emotions, nothing fills the need
Big fat pipes, stained spoons, and burners, twisted baco foil
Veins in tatters sunken eyes nothing left to spoil
Periodically she's anorexic occasionally she'll binge
One way traffic no escape route worships the syringe
Round and round in circles with a brain like bubble gum
This way that way scag head junkie pardon the sad pun
No rhyme no reason no firm plans from one second to another
No thoughts for others f — the hopes of friend or sister – mother
Can she make it? Will she break it? Evil nasty habit
She's caught within the headlights; pathetic, frightened rabbit.

She's A Junkie

My daughter's a junkie she's tempted to shout
In the midst of another meeting
Manages to stop herself blurting it out
Such a powerful feeling but fleeting
Worries each day from morning til night
Today will she just disappear?
Powerless feelings ideas are depleted
Can't stop her from getting the gear
Birds are singing, radios playing
Life seems so normal sublime
The letterbox rattles, it stares from the mat
Yet another parking fine
She stares at herself a face in the mirror

Tired and ravaged with worry
Must get to work and try to act normal
Desperate for the money
There hangs her photo on the wall in the hallway
Such an innocent quiet child
What made her do it she searches for reasons
As to why she should end up so wild
Some of her clothing litters the hallway
Brightly coloured and funky
She instructs herself "you must be strong now"
Mustn't shout out today "she's a junkie"

Emma sent me some more material to add to Addicts Language from the rehab centre. At the moment, even though she is finding it really hard, she's adamant she will stick it out and get clean. I made this poem up from the words used in what she sent me. It's entitled "If Only"

If Only

If only is a lonely place to be
For today we're not alone there's you and me
Walk the walk talk the talk
Let's have it right
Do as they suggest and win the fight
Reject denial and regression it's the way
No remorse means no recovery; just for today'
Work the programme check yourself discard the masks
You know your worth it get real with therapeutic tasks
Because today your not alone there's you and me
And if only is a lonely place to be

Addicts language

Drugs Are Evil

*D*isco biscuits, dope and draw
*R*ainbows, rugby balls
*U*ppers, Downers – useless life
*G*reen grass and gold dust calls
*S*kunk and skag and sweeties

*A*mphetamines and amps
*R*oofies, rock hard rollies ram and stomach cramps
*E*cstasy and eckies

*E*lephants, eggs and essence
*V*ile and sad crazy, none of
*I*t makes sense
*L*SD, lightening flash, love doves, liberties

*P*ractice
*A*ddicts language and
*Y*ou'll end up on your knees

Drugs are Such a Sin

Let's go on a trip, we can take my Mitsubishi
You can wear my Rolex, do you wanna try a mushie?
We can drive at a high speed
Young Charlie's coming too
Don't be a dope and chicken out
'C' sticks to me like glue
I swear you'll be in ecstasy
The weather forecasts snow
We'll buy some coke, roll on the grass
The weeds will grow and grow
Coz I'm a silly skag head
And you're my heroin
What a whiz what a crack
Drugs are such a sin.

Emma sent me this, it's an addicts lingo poem

```
    F I N E           F E A R           F E A R
    U N U M           U V N U           A V N E
    C S R O           C E D N           C E D C
    K E O T           K R                E R O
    E C T I           Y                        Y  V
    D U I O           T                        T  E
    R C N             H                    H   R
    E A        I                           I
    L               N                   N
                    G                       G

                  'DENIAL'

                 DON'T
                 EVEN
                 KNOW
                 I
                 AM
                 LYING
```

A Giant Step

Emma's first rehab

As I'm finishing Emma's story I am aware that she has taken a giant step towards getting clean.

Yesterday she went into rehab. I have promised her that I'll go to see her with her mum. If she does find the strength to stay there it will be for three months. She found on her interview that the rules and regulations there are very strict. Up at 7am they all share the household chores. She's about 200 miles from home and the rehab centre houses 28 recovering addicts. They are not allowed out for three weeks initially and then when they do go out, they are accompanied by five other people. During the day they attend meeting after meeting and this particular centre has a very good success rate. I spoke with Anne last night and she was both relieved and surprised that Emma had even agreed to stay there. She said that for her and the twins this was such and enormous relief, even if it didn't last the rest would do them all good. She also said that she'd lit a candle and prayed that her daughter would make it and I assured her that I would pray too. Now it's only a matter of time, but at least there's a tiny light at the end of her family's long dark tunnel. Emma has taught me not to judge anyone simply because through my own experience of knowing her she has proved that not all addicts are ruthless. Emma never took anything from me she only gave what she could to help me and my son.

I suppose you could call the NA meetings and the rehab a kind of brain washing, but at the end of the day this can only be seen as extremely positive and, having attended some, my advice to anyone who is really serious about getting clean is "Don't knock it until you've tried it" I have met many who have got clean and more importantly, stayed clean due to the solid support they have had from so many others.

Once again I struggled with how to end Emma's story, probably because it hasn't ended. I decided the best way is to use the last poem in her story. It's about a very recent conversation we had. As I've never sampled any illegal drugs in my life I was very curious as to what it feels like. Em told me exactly how it felt for her (in the beginning anyway) which is hopefully captured in this last work. At this point I will have to bore you with a little information on my own life. I have a comfortable home, a car, a small dog and an African grey parrot who is singing songs and talking to me as I write this. Like Emma I have a very good family. I do a lot of public speaking about mental health and have set up my own business 'Spotlight on Schizophrenia' in an attempt to educate the general public.

Due to poor media coverage, this is desperately needed. I enjoy my life, obviously it is still tinged with sadness. Getting back to my long conversation, Em said that she would rather be her than me. This shocked me, this talented, attractive young woman who openly admits that drugs have brought her to her knees still maintained that she was better off than me, so for me it was proof that addicts have a horrendously

distorted perception of life. Hopefully, "Rather me than you" will explain it more clearly. Finally, two questions
1) What will become of her?
2) Read the poem, compare her life to yours then ask yourself as I have, who would you rather be?

This was written after a conversation with Emma; she tried to explain what the attraction of drugs were for her, we write to each other frequently, I pray to God that she makes it.

Rather Me Than You

Devoid of all feelings or pressures of life
I can't see, can't hear, nothing's moving
Wrapped up in soft layers of cotton wool
White and fluffy and soothing
Cocooned in heroin's freedom transported away
From life's tomb
My brain closes down in an instant
As I wallow in the warmth of its womb
Engulfing my being, soothing my spirit
Warmth and softness and peace
Swimming through my well worn veins
Immediate freedom, relief
I can't hear the whining voices telling me to get clean
From a living waking nightmare
To a beautiful sensual dream
I drift on into oblivion, reality melting away
Magical freedom beckons me on
It's worth the high price that I pay
So you can call me scag head or junkie
In theory of course that is true
But wrapped up in the peace of my chemicals
I would rather be me than you.

Emma sent me some more material recently and I have used some of the sayings that they use in rehab for this next work. At the moment, although she says its tough, she is still adamant that she will make it and stay clean; her days are long and she attends meetings every day. She has now completed the first three steps of recovery with another nine to go.

Update: Emma had been in rehab for 11 weeks now, she remains clean, at least for today.

Further update 15th October 2003. Following 16 weeks Emma decided to come out of rehab at the weekend even though her family objected and tried hard to get her to stay. Her present whereabouts are unknown.

Chaz's Story

> Chaz; Aged 23; Started using heroin at the age of 15
>
> Method Of Feeding Habit: Thieving
>
> Uses in the arm or groin, will use anything but mainly heroin
>
> Hopes for the future: Getting clean
>
> Chaz (or 'The Hawk') went straight onto H at 15; did not have a clue what the tragic consequences would be (does now)
>
> Physical Description: Height 6ft 2ins Weight around 10 stone – teeth brown and disintegrating – very pronounced Adam's apple – walks with a permanent stoop. Overall appearance unkempt, but usually wears designer gear (he never pays for it). He describes what he does all day as "going to work"
>
> Chaz's mother Jean, school dinner lady – dad left when things began to get tough, was close to being an alcoholic himself.
>
> Home council flat but spends a lot of time in crack houses – what he hasn't stolen is bolted down (not that there's much left)
>
> Mother remains devoted even though he has robbed her of absolutely everything.

Chaz is not exactly your average junkie. He did not progress gradually apart from being a cannabis smoker from the age of 13, he hadn't dabbled in much else. He went for the biggie early on. Straight onto heroin at 15 years of age. His excuse for this little indiscretion—he was very good at football, in fact his dream was to be a pro. Chaz's hopes were shattered along with his right leg in a car crash, end of story – start of a life of depravity. The beginning of an 8-year nightmare to date.

Those years have certainly taken their toll on Chaz, his mother and their very meagre council flat. Chaz's father left as soon as things started to get tough. His mother didn't bat an eyelid; he was a very heavy drinker and bled her dry. So, if anything, when he disappeared into the night she silently breathed a sigh of relief. He constantly blamed her for the way that their son had turned out, even though he took no interest in the boy at all. Between the two of them, they had completely wrecked her life. I have never seen such a bare home as theirs; he had completely stripped it of everything. Every door had locks on, the TV was bolted down; too many had gone missing to take chances. One Sunday Chaz took everything out of the freezer to sell, even meat pies. His mother is old beyond her years and yet she still loves her son with all her heart and soul. Chaz's day begins as soon as the shops open. He calls what he does "going to work". He got his nickname through the way he perches on the railings watching and waiting for the unsuspecting shopkeepers to turn their backs. This is when "the hawk" swoops down for the pickings. They say that his timing is fantastic. Em told me that one afternoon he lifted 16 microwaves, the amazing part is that this was from the same store every time.

The Hawk

He perches on the railways on each relentless stalk
Swoops down for the pickings fearless is the hawk
Shiny ruffled feathers eyes as black as coal
He looks through you with a vengeance
That mirrors his black soul
His prey is blind to ruthlessness, the hawk must have his fill
He legs it fast and furious with the contents of the till
He rushes to the crack house oblivion at last
The syringe is now his closest friend blotting out the past
His nest is filled with replicas, losers, dealers, thugs
But the hawk has lost his freedom his wings now clipped by drugs

The Next Step?

Em told me that their whole week was spent going from one shop to another. Chaz would lift absolutely anything. There was always someone who would buy from him. Sometimes he would only get 10% of what the goods were worth—he was in no position to barter and the very fact that none of these things had cost him anything (money-wise) meant that he had no value for any of it. It didn't matter what something had cost—as long as he made enough money for his next hit, he was satisfied, in fact he was ecstatic. When his clothes got dirty he would go and get whatever he wanted including underwear, socks and aftershave, find the nearest public toilet and come out looking a lot smarter than he did when he went in. He would still look unshaven and unkempt as if he had only done half the job. The dirty clothes would be left in the bins. If he felt hungry he would walk around M+S (he liked their sandwiches) pick up a bottle of drink and a sandwich and devour them walking around the food hall. Em said that she believed he rarely got caught simply because he was so blasé about it. He really thought that it was his god-given right to just pick up whatever he fancied and eat it. This arrogance overrode any feelings of nervousness; he didn't even look guilty. Em said everyone liked Chaz with his pleasant ways and quiet demeanour, especially elderly people. She described him as kindness itself. At this moment in time Chaz manages to feed his habit and Emma's. She knows he can't keep this up as they are using more and more. She also knows that although she hasn't resorted to prostitution yet, even though the thought of it repulses her, it's probably the next step.

Scoring is about Chaz's mum. He even stole things from her that she treasured; she found this the hardest part of all, especially when he told he what he'd sold them for. This is what really made her realise how desperate her son had become. No one on this earth tried harder than her to help him. She talked to him until she was blue in the face. She supported him with her heart and her soul, he took everything she had. Her neighbours found her crying one morning; it transpired that Chaz had robber her freezer of everything that was in it. It included boxes of mince and onion pies that she'd got cheap. Nothing, absolutely nothing was safe when Chaz needed to score.

And so life goes on. 'The Hawk' still perches on the railings waiting to swoop; the only thing that changes is that this tragic young man sinks further and further into depravity. Case history two then comes to an end and we ask ourselves the burning question, "What will become of him?"

Again there is no answer; all I can say is that, judging by his appearance and from what Emma has told me about how much he is using (in his groin), it's very doubtful that Chaz will make old bones.

Scoring

His mother has aged twenty years while his habit has reached just eight
Each day she's engulfed in sadness sometimes she feels white-hot hate.
Robbed of a normal life, robbed of so many things
TVs, videos, hi fis, earrings, bracelets and rings
She's sick of his sad appearance; tired and worn down by his lies
Last week in his desperation he robbed her freezer for pies
It matters not who bought them; her treasured adored heirlooms
Cameo brooches and a large gold cross, stripped from barren wombs
She lights up another roll up her thirty-second today;
How will she afford the next pack she must try to find a way
He throws a new pack on the table nicked from the corner store
He mumbles this is for you mum then runs up to his room to score.

When Emma read "Scoring" she said that she'd seen Chaz throw that packet on the table "that's exactly how it is" she said.

His Pain

Microwaves and videos, mini chocolate bars
Pots and pans and paintbrushes, Bounty's Boosts and Mars
Hair gel, shampoo, tissues, cola, coco pops
Swift and sharp and cunning, a scourge to all the shops
He steals it for a living, to prevent his tragic hell
In carrier bags and under coats, anything will sell
Sports bags dresses shirts and ties trainers in a box
Jeans and jackets, after-shave, hankies, ties and socks
The dealers see him coming, pay a pittance for his wares
Devoured in an instant, no-one really cares
They laugh at what he stands for
They'd kick him in the gutter
Poor, sad, sorry loser
You'll often hear them mutter
He searches for a well-worn vein, immediate relief
No thought for tomorrow or his mother's grief
Another hit oblivion, so futile so insane
The devil's wretched advocate but nothing stops his pain.

Destined To Die Young

Addicts, scag heads, junkies, people with a need
Not satisfied with life's sweet plan, losers with a greed
Addicts, scag heads, junkie,s some are ruthless thru' and thru'
They'd steal your wallet for their next hit
Be careful, could be you
Addicts, scag heads, junkies, can't stand normality
They refuse to cope with pressures endured by you and me
Addicts, scag heads, junkies, at the bottom of life's rung
Arrogant, pathetic, tragic and destined to die young.

These were my thoughts on Chaz

This is the end of Chaz's story

> 15th October 2003: Chaz is still perching on the railings; his mother left that flat a few weeks ago.

Angie

> Nickname: Angel
>
> Age: 35
>
> Dependants: Three children all in care
>
> Mother: No contact, alcoholic
>
> Father: Unknown
>
> Partner, or Co-dependant: Joey, nicknamed "Geordie Boy", and also an addict
>
> Duration of habit: 18 years – 7 prison sentences
>
> Method of feeding habit: shoplifting and prostitution
>
> Situation now: still using
>
> Hope for the future: getting clean and getting her kids back

Angie doesn't wear a disguise, one small glance and you've got her sussed, her whole appearance spells **ADDICT.**

Small in stature, half of her teeth are missing, what's left are brown and disintegrating. Dark unkempt hair, sallow skin and very sad eyes. There appeared to be no depths Angie wouldn't sink to get her gear. Due to the amount of veins that have collapsed, she uses in the groin. All in all she's not what you'd call a pretty sight.

Angie was sexually abused by one of her many stepfathers. She did get to call this one daddy and says it was because he was around a bit longer than the others and that although he abused her, he had shown her some kindness. The more we talked, the more I believed her story, even though by this stage I realised that addicts are arch manipulators. All in all she'd spent about six years in women's prisons. Her longest stretch being 14 months and 14 months clean; the first phone call she made on each release was to—yes, you've guessed it—a dealer.

Even with her track record she firmly believes that one day she'll do it. She describes what it would be like to get her kids back and live a normal life. Her biggest worry, apart from where her next hit is coming from, is that one of her kids follows the same path as she has. Her mother is an alcoholic who was just as bad as she was. She can remember her being in a drunken stupor for days on end. Angie and her two younger brothers (one of whom is an addict) learned from a very early age how to fend for themselves. At the age of 13 and following five years of abuse, Angie found the courage to tell her mother the truth. Her mother blamed her saying she enticed him by the clothes that she wore.

Angie is a self-harmer. Her arms are covered in small cuts. The only thing—apart from cutting her arms to ribbons—that helps her deal with the horrors of her childhood is taking heroin. Out of all the females I have talked to, she has too many reasons to be free from pain to be blamed for the plight she found herself in.

Secrets

I hear your footsteps on the stairs
I should really be asleep
You press a finger on my lips
Saying "this is our secret to keep"
I pray you won't hurt me quite so much
As you invade my space
I tell myself fairy stories
I try hard not to look at your face

Next morning at school my teacher is kind
I long to tell her what's wrong
I hear your voice "it's our secret
You must always try to be strong"

But I always thought secrets were wonderful things
My minds eye saw beautiful scenes
But our secret is nothing like that at all
You shattered my wonderful dreams

At last you tip toe out of my room
Our secret safe once again
I know I will never tell anyone
But how do I cope with the pain

Princess

Please don't call me your princess, call me Angie instead
I don't feel much like a princess when you force your way into me bed
Why do you call me your princess when you make me feel dirty and sad
I don't understand what you do to me
But somehow I know that it's bad
A princess lives in a castle, amongst beautiful magical things
She's surrounded by love and affection
Necklaces, bangles and rings
She doesn't cry like I do, her family is loving and kind
She's not tainted by pure evil, forever searching her mind
A princess will marry her prince one day
She doesn't end up with the baddie
So try not to call me princess
And I'll try not to call you daddy.

Angie says that all addicts have been bitten by a vampire, which was what made me write "Vampire's Gear"

Vampire's Gear

She's been bitten by a vampire, he prodded, he probed, and then he sucked
Living a life of depravity, at 35 she's f*****
With no plans for the future, drained of life's sweet blood
The first bite took her into oblivion

Then sent her back down with a thud
Just one bite then she was his servant
Pasty pallor, bloodshot eyes
Facing a life of sheer misery, no escaping her tragic disguise
Three children robbed of their mother with each of them living in care
Born without love and affection to a world that's so unfair
She wakes from a fitful sleep and plans each tedious day
Stares hard at her haggard appearance, how on earth did it get this way?
So remember beware of the vampire, don't be tempted to think "what the heck?"
He hides furtively in every corner, ready to bite a new neck
He'll rob you of any true feelings as he draws out your life's blood
You'll be branded scag head and junkie
Just another joke in the pub
Don't be dragged down into his underworld
Don't let him get too near
Don't sell your soul to the devil
Don't sample the vampire's gear.

Sold

Abused by a man she called daddy
No respite for this little
Girl
Innocence
Ebbing away each night

Ongoing pain, head's a whirl
Regaining self worth an impossible task, yet

Princess tries hard to stay sane
Resigned to a life filled with sadness she
Instructs herself "deal with the pain"
Needless to say Angie found her escape through heroin crack and speed, At last sweet relief from her
Endless hell, drugs fulfil her every need

Addicts language

Secrets, secrets, secrets, secrets must never be told
   a princess destroyed by pure evil, a life to the devil
Sold

This is the end to Angies story.

> 15th October 2003: the last thing I heard about Angie is that she's been in hospital because she's covered in lumps and one of her legs is swollen to twice the size of the other.

It's strange how history has a habit of repeating itself. Angie told me that she can vividly remember her mother being in a drunken stupor sometimes for days on end. She was often carted off by social workers, kicking and screaming, to be taken to yet another foster home, never happy in any. She does admit that she didn't exactly make their lives easy, quite the reverse. She often absconded and more often that not made her way back home, such as it was. Her own three were destined to follow the same route. In and out of homes while she did time for thieving or receiving with intent to supply drugs; they were shifted about from pillar to post and yet they loved their mother unconditionally and would protect her to the bitter end. One thing I will say about Angie is that, apart from Joey, she really was alone; she said that she envied Emma because Emma did have a good family who were always willing to support her. Again, I couldn't help wondering whether it really would have made any difference or was this purely another excuse for the fact that she didn't have enough willpower to beat drugs.

Yet again another story with no end. Well, what conclusion have you come to? Now that you've read Angie's story, do you believe that she will ever get her kids back? Or do you think that she will sink even further down, not that there's much further to go. I'm sure you heart goes out, as mine does, to this tragic young woman and I'm also sure that your head is saying, "I wouldn't lay bets on it".

Angie And Her Inner Light

The first thing that struck me about Angie is that she had no "inner light". Just as if someone had flicked the switch.

On the streets by the age of 18 to pay for her craving for drugs
She mixes with low life losers, dealers and thugs
She says the worst part's the smell, the one's that are none too clean
She'd much rather deal with an ugly one; its hard to imagine the scene
She's abused to feed her habit just like a human spittoon
Her favourites are the premmies, the ones where it's over soon
She shoves the notes down her bra muttering poor sad sod
Tells herself that was the last time cross her heart she swears it to God
Her inner voice mocks till the next time that the craving proves far too strong
Give her two days at the most then correct me if I'm wrong
She showers vigorously to try to get rid of the smell
The first time she laughed and sampled a joint began her journey to hell
Jesus Christ the horror of drugs there's far more to life than this
There's decency and happiness instead of a deep dark abyss.
But for her there's misery and craving, there's sunken bloodshot eyes
There's depression as bad as it gets, along with a few phoney highs
Once she was really attractive, she was lively vivacious and bright
Till the day she decided to sample some pot then out went her inner light.

A very powerful love affair

One of the mothers that I interviewed told me that, about three years into her daughter's addiction, she found a few letters that her daughter had written. At first she thought that they were love letters, but when she started to read them she realised to her horror that they were letters her daughter had penned to her drugs, yet another indication of how hard it must be to get clean, I wrote this after our conversation.

'My lover my hero-in'

I love you because you're kind to me
You help to ease my aching soul
I love you for the way you help
To fill this gaping hole
I know you're always there for me
You never let me down
A friend that I can call on
In this god-forsaken town
I love the way you ease the pain
I feel from day to day
I reach out so many times for you
You help me to find a way
To escape from all the hurt inside
And find real peace at last
You blot out painful memories
From my futile wasted past
The price I pay is worth it
You understand the pain I'm in
I'll love you till the day I die
My hero, heroin.

Joey's Story

> Nickname: Geordie Boy
>
> Age: 36
>
> Started using: 16
>
> Parents: No contact devastated by the situation
>
> Married at 18: 2 children, no contact with either of them
>
> Situation now: still using
>
> Hopes for the future: getting clean and contact with his kids again
>
> Physical Description: 5ft 8" weight around 9 stone, wiry skinhead; body piercing, tattoos, Joey's favourite tattoo is "H" for happiness.

Out of all of them, Joey felt the most guilt. His parents prayed for a son, the youngest of five, Joey was the only boy. He says he can never forgive himself for the pain he has caused to his family and his wife and kids. One by one he lost them all. Joey said if he ever manages to stay clean, he is not sure how he will cope with the guilt. I couldn't help thinking, "Well that's as good an excuse as any." He and Angie met in rehab, each says that they don't know how they would cope without the other. So where and how did it all start to go wrong? He changed so much—they racked their brains as to why and how.

To say that Joey was a nightmare would be an understatement. He became very aggressive and seemed to delight in getting into scrapes. The more his family nagged the worse his behaviour got. He rebelled against everything and everybody. His father tried everything to tame him to no avail. It was as if he delighted in living up to all the names the family called him. They even paid a counsellor; after three fruitless sessions with Joey refusing point blank to say a word, they told him not to bother coming back. The signs were there. The counsellor told his parents that he was concerned about the carved heads that Joey had made. He'd spent hours chiselling tiny pieces of wood off them. At one of the sessions out of sheer boredom Joey had stormed out of the room refusing to speak. He picked three of them up to look at them more closely and noticed that although they were meticulously carved none of them had a mouth. They all had eyes, nose, ears, hair but no mouth. When he told Joey's parents, they said he had never discussed his grandmother's death with anyone. So, he progressed from bad to worse. By the age of 13 he had quite a bad habit as far as cannabis was concerned. His parents were totally at a loss as to which way to turn with him. The little time he was indoors was spent in his bedroom spending hours carving wood. His father ranted and raved, his sisters mostly gave him a very wide berth or lectured him on the way he treated his parents. His mother cried, she cried buckets and tried endlessly to rack her brain as to where they had gone wrong. By the time he reached 15, Joey was totally out of control. His parents really thought that they had been through the worst; little did they know that compared to what lay ahead this was child's play. His parents say that although they didn't see it at the time, things started to go wrong after the death of his grandmother.

Life's Pains

Joey was 12 years old when she died. He went round to see her after school one afternoon. The front door was open and her neighbour was standing in the hall clutching a handkerchief. She bent down and took both of his hands looking right into his eyes. She said very slowly and quietly, "Joey, I want you to run an errand for me son, I want you to go home a fetch your mam. He wanted to say "but I want to see my grandmother first" but something told him that something was terribly wrong and that he had to do exactly as she asked him to do. He never saw her again and found it so hard to accept that he'd never hear her voice or feel her plump cool arms around him ever again. He even missed her smell, she wore that loose powder and he loved the smell of it. Joey was never the same after her death, he'd sit for hours talking about the times they'd spent together. He'd laugh when he remembered the check cap she'd bought him, and how she'd pinch his cheeks. Secretly he hated wearing it and as soon as he got round the corner he'd whip it off and look round to see if any of his mates had seen him in it. He'd stuff it in his back pocket feeling a bit guilty; he refused to go to the funeral and felt guilty about that too. Joey's schoolwork deteriorated but he didn't seem to care. His parents were forever up at the school about his truancy; they were aware of the change in him but, in a hectic household and with four teenage girls to worry about, other matters took priority. None of them really knew how much he missed his gran or how much it had effected him.

Talking to Joey one thing is certain, he feels he's let her down; she'd lectured him so many times on how to conduct his life, talked to him for hours about taking care of the people who mattered. How could he have made such a huge mistake? We talked endlessly about not being able to turn back the clock and the fact that we all made mistakes and how beating himself up for past mistakes was not the answer, nor was it what she would have wanted. Joey said that if he stopped taking drugs, he wouldn't be able to deal with his guilt. I couldn't help thinking yet again, is that just another excuse? Yet again another question with no answer. How is it that people can go through the most dreadful things and manage to cope while others turn to drugs? Joey says he's just one of those people who can't deal with life's pains.

Life's Pains

Please don't judge me for being a junkie
I'm well aware that my future's in tatters
I also know it's a senseless path
And I've lost all the people that mattered
I know I'm pathetic and useless
Do you think I don't know what I've lost
My home, my respect and my future
So I'm well aware of the cost.
I know I must find the strength one day
To fight off the demons within
I've lost count of the times that I've tried in the past

So tenacious and determined to win
I've beaten temptation before
Resisted the heat of the fire
Stared hard in the face of a normal existence
Then slowly slipped back in the mire
Please don't judge me for being a junkie
Don't stare at my broken down veins
At the end of the day you are stronger than me
You have managed to deal with 'life's pains'

Wasted Advice

Precious Youth

Understand the meaning of life Joey
My grandmother used to say
Though she loved me she'd turn in her grave
If she could see me today
Live your life to the full Joey
But be good to the people who care
When times get tough remember this
Only a few will be there
I miss her with my heart and soul
Thank God she can't see what I am
She tried so hard to show me the way
This life that I'm living's a sham
It's best she believes she got through to me
She wasn't meant to know the truth
That I never did learn the meaning of life
And I've wasted my precious youth

How Joey Feels: "I'm Sorry"

I know you expected more of me
And how you both prayed for a son
I know you've done your best for me
Dutiful father and loving mum
I don't expect your forgiveness
I'm sick of you taking the blame

I let you all down with the rehab
My behaviour has caused you such shame
My sisters have always been good to you
It's me who has burst your bubble
Joy riding, thieving, drink and drugs
From the age of twelve, I was trouble
Mum's crying and twisting her handkerchief
Asking me where they went wrong
Five kids you've brought up together
God knows you've had to be strong
I know you deserved so much more from me
For years I've been such a worry
What can I say? I'm a failure
But I'm sorry—I'm truly sorry.

Joey had got clean once, in fact he was clean for over a year. He got himself a job as a hod carrier on a building site. The work dried up and it was a case of last in first out. It was as if the work helped him to stay clean and, once it was gone, with it went his determination. With little to do all day he started smoking cannabis—end of being clean. Unlike the others, Joey doesn't run on about getting clean again; his motto is "keep quiet if you're not sure if you can do it". Due to his terrible guilt, I doubt Joey will ever make it. If he did it would mean facing his demons. Dealing with the past, he finds it easier to blot it out and drugs are the answer to oblivion.

Roll On Bloody Death

"Roll on bloody death" those four words are the final words in Joey's story. Joey actually said that one day, 36 years old with a lifetime left to live, but this was his attitude to life. A friend of mine died from cancer at the age of 34 a few years ago. I will never forget her iron will and determination to live. She got married in hospital three days before she died, her strength was awe-inspiring; this was not going to beat her but beat her it did. I wondered how she would have felt if she'd heard Joey; yet another example of the power that drugs have over us;

another reason to avoid them like the plague. What a tragic attitude at 36 years old.

Roll On Bloody Death

Broken down veins like road maps
Eyes sunken deep in his head
Dark shadows lurking beneath them
And a stomach that's rarely fed
The room looks like a tip strewn with super brew cans
It reeks of sheer futility – just like his well-laid plans
He dreams of his wife and kids, a semi in a tree-lined street
But he hasn't a pot to piss in or decent shoes on his feet
He steals from the houses he dreams of to pay for the ecstasy
Along with the smack and the heroin; God will he ever be free?
He drags himself up from the mattress muttering under his breath
Time to go on a trip and "roll on bloody death"

This is the end of Joey's Story
    Update 15th October 2003 Joey is still using

Trudie's Story

Trudie's story is the worst-case scenario. Trudie paid the ultimate price for her addiction, the price of death. She's left behind sadness beyond compare, a mother who blames herself, a brother who feels angry, a father who openly admits that due to the effect that drug addiction has had on all of their lives, when her heard about her death along with all the other emotions, he also felt a certain amount of relief because he now knew that her relentless suicide was over and she was at peace at last. And last but not least, drugs have robbed her seven-year-old son of his mother. Her story is shorter than the rest like her time on earth; the work is based on the conversations I had with her grieving family who are understandably still feeling their loss.

Trudie

> Trudie: 26; Dependent is her son, Liam aged 7. Liam's father is unknown but Nigerian.
>
> Trudie's mother is Jane, a schoolteacher. Father is a GP, Geoff. James, her brother, is studying English literature at university.
>
> Duration of habit: 9 years on heroin
>
> Method of feeding: Prostitution
>
> Situation now: Died in February last year from an overdose.

On the surface this family had the lot. Well they did up until Trudie started taking drugs, progressing from cannabis, amphetamines, crack cocaine and finally heroin. Her dad was so anti-drug owing to the fact that he had zipped up too many body bags containing corpses. She was the apple of his eye and he was devastated to find that his daughter had become a junkie. He can recall saying to the paramedics as he zipped up the bag for yet another junkie "my son is at uni', I hope he never gets hooked". The work is based on conversations we had.

Addicts language

How James feels:

Poxy Drugs

Junkies they're so pathetic
Take a look at my mum and dad
Even worse take a look at her son
He's an orphan now poor lad
She's mucked up so many lives
Now they're left to bring up her child
She shirked her responsibilities
From the age of 16 she was wild
Sorry I can't feel any pity
Even though you might think that I'm wrong
She's left me to pick up the pieces
And what with uni, I have to stay strong
She's not here to hear Liam crying
We all know he's missing the hugs
Druggies, they make me so angry
This is all down to poxy drugs

A Taste
(GP talking to paramedic)

Life extinct the GP said, zipping up the bag
Move him to the mortuary and don't forget the tag
Rigour set in hours ago, Jesus drugs are vile
I'd put his death around midnight
He's been gone for quite a while

Overdosed without a doubt it was still in the vein
I pulled it out; I'd put his age round seventeen
What a tragic waste
My boy's at university
Hope he don't get a taste.

Mother Blames Herself

Call myself a teacher? I suppose it's good for a laugh
I've let you down so badly, no time for you in the past
Possessions were top of my list supplying our every need
As I watch them lower your coffin down
I'm engulfed by the guilt of my greed

He holds on so tight to my hand, my grandson, your darling boy
I'll be the teacher he needs now, I won't palm him off with a toy
If only, if only, if only, if only, I'd taught you instead
If only I'd steered you away from drugs then you wouldn't have ended up dead

Poor Sad Sod

She convinces herself that it's a game
She instructs herself to be strong
Twenty quid that's enough for a hit
And it doesn't last very long
She clenches her fists and her teeth
As they make their way to the bed
He can do what he wants to my body
But he'll never get into my head
It's over in a flash; she whispers "thank you God"
He stuffs two tenners down into her boots
She smiles thinking "poor, sad sod"

Liam's situation
Off in a dream

He stares at her coma like state
Slowly rocks her with his small hand
"Wake up mummy, I'm hungry" too young to understand
"Wake up mummy, I'm thirsty" he rocks her gently again
The tears mist up in his eyes, "Wake up, lets play that new game"
But mummy's off in oblivion, wrapped up tight in her cocoon
The ashtrays are overflowing
In their ever darkened room
He'd love to go to McDonalds, Billy from school always goes
His mummy drives a BM and wears only the smartest clothes
He'd love a mummy like Billy's, he envies his clothes they're so clean
Wake up mummy I'm hungry, but mummy's off in a dream.

Be A Good Lad; *Trudie to Liam*

She touches his tight black curls, as guilt takes over her being
She hates the fact she's a junkie, she can't bear what he's seeing
She's aware she should set an example; she should kick her habit for good
She gazes into his trusting brown eyes, God if only she could
She begins applying her make up, each day it's a harder task
He watches every move she makes and then finally he asks
"Where are you going to mummy?" "Are you going to work again?"
"We can't live on thin air Liam" it causes her so much pain
"One day mummy won't have to work when she meets and marries her prince"
Her first client is fat and balding; the thought of it makes her wince
If only he'd heard about hygiene, then it wouldn't be quite so bad
"Why do you have to go mummy?" "Take this fiver, now be a good lad"

Safe And Sound
Father's thought at the funeral

As they lower you into the ground, I throw in a blood red rose
Your mother throws in a handful of earth, sobbing and blowing her nose
My mind drifts back through the years to the apple of my eye
I'm sobbing uncontrollably though I promised not to cry
Many times we brought you back home, sorely neglected and thin
Hauled you out of another crack house, Christ what a state you were in
As they lower you into the earth with people crying all around
I breath a sigh of relief, at last you're safe and sound.

Trudie's Story – Conclusion

This story of course did have an end, a very tragic end. Her mother said that she doesn't know how she will ever forgive herself for not warning Trudie on the dangers of drugs (as if it would have made a difference). Even as I am writing these words, a nagging inner voice taunts me by saying what possible difference do you honestly think all this copious writing will make? So, what drives me on? The enormity of this problem is the answer to that. The pain and suffering that it causes. Only last night I had a long conversation with Emma's sister (case history 1) she rang to ask me if I'd heard from Em. She asked me if I thought it would be worth her while finding her. She said that she knew that short of putting her in chains she would simply be wasting her time. And so it goes—on more and more heartache. As for Trudie's family, they tell me that Liam is their saviour in all this. The child that they had begged their daughter to abort is now a living testament to her memory and has become their reason for living. One thing's for sure, this young lad will not be short of lectures about drug addiction. They assure me that they will do everything in their power to stop him from following the same path as his mum.

Liam will be one young man at least who will never be tempted (their words), or will he?

This is the end of Trudie's story

A Success Story At Last

Tony

> Tony Marsh
>
> Age: 30
>
> Physical Description: Height: 5'11"
>
> Weight: around 13 Stone
>
> Hair: Dark, cropped
>
> Tattoos, some gold teeth
>
> Tanned and muscular
>
> Tony was a self-harmer and has white slash marks on his lower arms.
>
> Tony is a picture of physical fitness
>
> Situation now: Own flat, car, painting and decorating business; clean for almost two years
>
> Hopes for the future: Staying clean and to continue helping others and enjoying his life.

As part of his rehab programme, Tony was asked to write his life story. These are Tony's words and he has kindly given me permission to publish them as part of this book in the hope that lessons will be learned from his horrendous past. His story is both shocking and tragic; it is also very powerful and there are many lessons to be learned from it. The biggest of all is that it can be done, but only if you share his tenacity, his strength and iron will.

Tony's Life Story—Maybe Tomorrow

One

My name is Anthony William Marsh. I was born in Greenwich hospital on 21st June 1973. I have a sister named Tina who is two years older than me. I did` have an older brother who died at six months old. My mother was pregnant with me when he died. When I was 6 months old my mother left home—to this day, I don't know why. But by the time I was six years old, I was feeling very insecure and angry. I felt hurt that I didn't have a mother. By the time I was around six I was already blaming myself for being born. I thought that if I'd never been born my mother, father and sister would be living a very happy life. My father helped to cement these beliefs by telling me that he wished he'd never had me and that he also wished that my brother was still alive. I felt guilty and would try all the time to make it up to my sister and father. No matter what I did it was wrong; my father gave my sister everything, I got fuck all.

I was screaming inside, no one to turn to, no one to hold me, no one to be nice to me. I thought I was odd in every way. I hated everyone, my father, my sister, my friends. I wanted to cry, but if I got tearful my father would tell me what a wimp I was and how if my brother was alive, he'd sort me out with a good kicking.

I was so lonely I'd go to bed and pray that my mum would come home. It would make things better, I needed her, she was my mother, where was she? I wanted her to hold me and tell me everything would be ok.

At the age of seven, my father had me going out stealing. I liked it at first, I felt needed by my old man. He would use the money for drink and for food. He'd say "well done son" which meant so much to me. As this was the only time he'd say it, when I went to school I'd make the other kids play 'penny up',

I'd take the money home, it made my dad happy and that made me happy. I would get hit for no reason. One day at school I stole a teacher's handbag. They caught up with me in the playground, I wouldn't give it up and threw it onto the roof. They called my father and he came to the school. In the office my father was both sorry and supportive. At home he took his belt to me, it rained blow after blow on my backside shouting, "haven't I taught you anything you stupid little c***, how the fuck did you get caught?" I felt so bad about letting him down, I'd only stolen it so as to have a good night with him.

I so wanted my mother, I wanted to be like to kid next door. He was so happy with his mother. Apart from the pain I felt so alone. The pain made me feel as if a nurse was with me, it was comforting and I'd hold onto my body parts yet this pain was a comfort. It gave my gut and heart comfort as they were in just as much pain as me. It made me think that there was two of us in pain, connected somehow.

If anyone pissed my dad off, it would come back to me. In my child's mind I thought this was alright as I didn't feel so alone. I loved my dad so much that no matter what he did it was all right by me. One night I came home to find yet another new woman there. They were both pissed and falling all over the place. My dad called her over and gave her a love bite on her neck. Then he told her to fetch him a drink. When she came back in the room he saw the love bite and asked her how she'd got it. He beat her up. I'd seen him do it, but I was too scared to open my mouth. It hurt me and made me feel so sad. I wanted my mum where was she? I was so confused.

From the age of seven, I would spin round and round in circles just to feel intoxicated and get away from the confusion in my head. It made me feel happy and light-headed, no worries. I'd fall over and it would hurt, but I would enjoy the hurt. I was a young boy craving love and attention and I would do anything to get it.

I was nicking bubble gum machines, anything I could get my hands on for my dad. My dad's friend Rushedy always paid me attention. He'd play games with me, he had time for me. If he saw me out with my friend he'd stop and talk to us. I liked and trusted him, he ended up physically and sexually abusing me in ways that made me feel dirty and guilty. I felt even more alone. I didn't have the guts to tell anyone. I hated my dad for not being there, I really needed my mum, where was she? I cried in my room for days, my anger would come and I wanted to die. I was so scared, I felt so ashamed of myself. I felt as if I was less than any other kid in the world. So scared, I was filled with real fear. I couldn't sit down normally, I just wanted to stay in bed, but my father got me out of bed to go. I hated him for it.

At school I had my power back by beating up another kid. I wouldn't stop hitting him. One morning it took three teachers to pull me off him, for once in my young life I felt good. This was the first time I'd felt power and control and I loved it.

When my dad found out he hit me, but also said "well done" afterwards, that made me feel nice. I was still so lost I made up an invisible mum; she'd tell me nice things and listen to me.

I started drinking my dad's booze at night to sleep. It helped with my bed-wetting. By now I was trying every way I could to earn money for my dad. He'd take me to the shops and put things in my pockets. When we were clear of the shops, he'd tell me how good I was at it.

By the age of eight, I'd got everyone's handwriting down to a 't'. When I handed my work in my teacher would say "who wrote it for you today then?" I did it because I wanted to be that other kid that day. I was in so much pain in my own lonely world I wanted help. I'd say "mum please help me" I really believed she was helping me because I was getting through the days.

By now I was really confused; I felt jealous of my sister and even more jealous of my dead brother. If only, if only, I needed him to be alive and then my mum and dad would like me. I'd be just like all of the other kids. I hated myself for letting Rashedy do that to me, even though I said "no"; I hated not pleasing my dad. I hated not liking my sister, why me? Why me?

At eight to nine, I had power and control over other kids. I took whatever I wanted from them, but I didn't ever think of them as people who had feelings of pain like me. So what I did was ok. I'd ask my dad for a mouthful of his booze, I'd put some in my bike bottle. I was nicking more and more, bikes, wheels, brakes; I'd sell them to kids on our block and other blocks. I'd give my dad some of the money and I kept some for myself. I hated my dad's drinking; he had a few women friends by now, and I hated them too. In fact I hated anyone who was close to my dad and yet I wanted to tell him, but I never did and that made me even more angry. I played the joker; I was so scared that other kids would see the truth. To help myself I'd either hurt them or laugh at them.

Around nine, my friends were all two or three years older them me. I liked a girl named Tina Wilson; she lived on my block. I made out I was 12 because my mates had girlfriends. She made me feel cool and at ease. We started kissing and feeling each other up. I didn't like her touching me, but I loved touching her. It felt good to tell my mate what I was doing with her. I was 'Jack the lad', I was part of something.

At nine, my dad called me in one day and said that my mum wanted to see me and my sister. My father had that cold unpredictable look in his eyes. I didn't like that look I was scared of it. I didn't know whether to cry, run, or kick the table. I couldn't believe that I was going to see her. We both started to cry, my old man said, "you don't have to see her", what a joke, I was crying with relief that my mum wanted to see me at last. I couldn't believe it; I was also very frightened that she wouldn't like me. Then my dad dropped the bombshell, with a big smile he said "she's got two other kids, a boy and a girl" I hated him for saying it but within half an hour I thought "that's cool, they're young and I'll be able to control them. The next day I told my friends about it. I was scared but at the same time I couldn't wait. In my head I saw her as tall, blond, pretty with bright eyes and a big smile. The morning went really slow, I stayed in my room. I didn't want to go out with my friends. I didn't have to go to Deptford market or the shops looking for her, looking for someone that I didn't know. A few days before this my dad had hit me with a pencil in his hand, it had gone into my ear and it really hurt for days. On that morning he told me to take a bath. In the bath I was talking to my mum and she was talking back to me.

I was sad, then happy, then excited. At times I was laughing, it felt pukka. When I got out of the bath there were new clothes laid out on the bed. I couldn't believe it, I was going to look nice for my mother. I can remember really thanking my dad, he seemed different for some reason I didn't understand. He sat me down and started talking to me, yes to me! I couldn't really understand what he was trying to say. He said "tell her you're happy and doing well at school, say everything is good for you, have a good time, take this phone number and if you don't like her call me". I didn't say this but I felt as if I'd known her all my life. "I love her dad, I do like her". It hurt him saying this but all I said was "OK, I will"; I felt sad and confused.

When I first saw her she came to the house. I was scared because my dad didn't say a word. I could see by his face that he hated her. She was prettier than I had imagined, tall blond with a very soft voice, but I didn't know her, it didn't feel right. She said "hello". I said "don't touch me!" without even saying it. My sister was OK with her, we got to her house in Grove Park. I was pleased that I knew where she lived now.

Inside the house we met two happy kids and her husband Jimmy. I liked him he was funny and made me laugh. Jackie (my mum) sat down beside me and asked me about school. I sure felt odd, didn't really want to talk to her. She took us all to the park, my sister played with her kids, I played alone. Jimmy sat with me and tried to make me laugh, I didn't want to be there.

We all went back to her house, I hated it, I didn't want to be there, and I started on her kids. I could see that it hurt her so I did it all the more. I kicked off saying that my ear hurt and that her kids had done it. She rang my dad, he was pissed. Too pissed to pick me up.

So my dad's mate Steve met me at the hospital, Steve was very understanding. He told me everything would be all right. He seemed to understand me even though I wasn't talking. He took me home, Tina was out and dad was in one of his horrible moods. I went to bed although I didn't want to be alone, I felt so unwanted.

The next day dad was in a good mood. I asked where my sister was and he said "with your mother" I felt jealous, I nicked a Tenants from the fridge even there was only two in there. I felt really sick and then he asked me where his drink had gone. He started hitting me when I said I didn't know. "lying little bastard" he said "what have I always told you?" "nick off of them c****s out there, not off your dad, I'll teach you". I ran off that day thinking I'd never go back again only to find myself back in my garden that night. Every time I went back I thought that things would get better, but they never did. The next day I ran away for a long time.

I finally went back and my dad had had a heart attack. I was 11 years old. I hated him laying there with all those tubes and machines, useless. He couldn't get out of bed, it scared me. I really felt for him, he wasn't pissed and he said that things would change, they didn't.

I started on gas and glue, it made me feel brave and it took away my sadness and loneliness. My mates didn't seem to love it as much as I did. I'd even nick it, I wanted it all the time. I stopped going to school, just stopped. I couldn't be bothered to hop the wag. Still using gas and glue I started to use cannabis. I'd nick car cassettes from cars, any car, my friends saw me being beaten up. This bloke caught me at his car, they didn't help so I beat them both up. My mates said I was mad, I liked it and did it all the more.

Stix and Stones

Two

My nickname was 'Sticks' because I'd carry a stone and a stick and play a game called dance. If they wouldn't dance I'd hit them with it. It was because I either didn't like them or was jealous of them.

My dad had another heart attack. A social worker came to the hospital and said I'd have to go into care 'til he got better. I didn't understand and felt as if I was being punished. I hated this lady and told her to piss off. I was really scared, I ran off and bought some glue. I felt brave again and went back to the hospital. Dad said I'd have to go with her. I hated him for it, why didn't he want me no more? Fuck 'em all, I went to the loo and did some more glue. They took me to a kid's home in Deptford; there was ten kids there, girls and boys. I was real scared when I walked in there. The girls all liked Billy, he was hard. I remember thinking if he was hard I'd be harder. Billy seemed to like me; I was so scared, I wanted my mum or my dad or sister to come and see me, at least one of them. Next morning at breakfast I was like the new kid on the block. The others seemed to find it funny. I didn't like the staff—there was something about them. I was eating my toast and the kids started telling me this scary story. One of Billy's mates told me to move; he said it was his seat not mine. I was scared to move and yet scared not to. I told him to go away, he went mad at me and we started fighting. It was as if my dad was in my head. I could see him clearly, it felt like if I didn't "do" him, my dad wouldn't be happy. It took four of the staff to break us up. Billy followed me upstairs and said "well done Tony". The other kid came into the room and we started fighting again. Billy tried to stop us so I ended up fighting with him. It ended up with me hitting Billy with a clock radio. They both ended up crying, I loved it, I felt so powerful.

Over the next few weeks all the girls seemed to like me, and me and Billy became good mates. We took money and sweets, whatever we wanted. Still I hated it there, I ran away and went to see my dad in hospital. I told him how much I hated it. He asked me about the other kids I told him they were all scared of me. When I told him about the fights he laughed and said "that's my boy, that's how I trained you" I felt proud of myself.

One of the care workers came and took me back. I was still using gas, glue, puff and air fresheners, me and Billy were on it all the time. I'd been there about six or seven weeks and one afternoon one of the care workers was trying to play a game with me. He tried to touch my bum like Rushedy did. I went mad and stabbed him in the hand; it was because I was so frightened. He told the other staff I'd done it for nothing. I couldn't believe it, they wanted to call the police. In the end they moved me to another house in Milton Keynes. I hated it even more. I hated the way they spoke and the clothes they wore.

I ran away to London on the streets for about two weeks. I was with other older kids who were well into glue and puff. I went back to my dad's house; he was out of hospital. I was happy with the thought of seeing him, when I knocked on the door I felt real scared. When he opened the door I cried, it's the first time I ever remember him cuddling me. He said it would be alright, I started to cry again I didn't seem to be able to stop. He told me to be strong and went back to his drink. I got angry and asked him why I couldn't come home. He didn't answer, just kept on drinking. He gave me a roll up, I didn't know what to do, he started laughing and said he knew I smoked. Even though I wasn't sure whether to light it or not just in case he hit me, I lit it and he didn't–see Tony, your dad does love you!!!

About three hours later he started going mad again. He had another unknown woman in the house, she ran out holding her face. I knew he'd hit her and told myself it was probably her fault anyway. By now I was scared about what might come my way. I went to my room, he called me down and asked if I had any money, I gave him what I had, he wasn't happy and he started on me. I kicked an ashtray over just to

get it over with, it ended up with him hitting me so much I didn't think the punches would ever stop. I really thought I was going to die this time. I was in so much pain when he finally stopped I started laughing. I knew how much he hated it. He started kicking me. I was on the floor, he shouted "get out you little bastard! Get up and get out!" I thought I'd run to London again on the streets. My arm and my chest hurt so much I was in bits. I hobbled out of the house only to find myself in the back garden yet again a few hours later. Exhausted I fell asleep and woke up in even more pain. I needed help so badly but I didn't know who to ask.

Finally the police picked me up. They rang the home in Milton Keynes, back I went again. I had to see the doctor, I told them I'd fallen off my bike, I didn't even have one. I'd got a broken arm and two broken ribs. He made me wear this thing across my chest. The care worker turned up, I didn't want her near me it was all her fault in the first place.

So it was back to Milton Keynes again, new kid on the block. Again 20 other kids, no glue, no puff, no nothing. As soon as I got back I was back on the air freshener again. I laid in the dorm which I shared with eight other kids. I was 12 years old now, nothing had changed for me, hitting other kids, fighting more and more coz I felt like it. Everyone was puffing and drinking. I liked it, we were all naughty kids I was the worst but that was what made me feel better. I got kicked out for pushing a teacher down the stairs; I don't even know why I did it, I must have been out of my nut.

The kids home didn't like it and asked why I'd done it. They told me that my care worker was coming to see me and that I had to stay in for them, fuck that and fuck them, I went out laughing and feeling good about myself. I went on like this until my care worker said "Tony, this ain't working, we've set up a family for you to live with in Catford. I felt hurt, new kid on the block again. More fights and even more shit, lonely again without my mates, everything was gone again, my mates, my power. I didn't even like leaving Milton Keynes, back to my dad's manor. When I went into the house I thought "here we go again". The family was black which was OK, they seemed really friendly. I had a 14 year old with me and we'd nick from houses, warehouses and shops. I loved the power it gave me and I loved the buzz of doing it. I had loads of fights that year, I was puffing constantly and would only ever go a few days without a puff or gas. My mate gave me a trip, now that **was** nice. I loved the powerful feeling it gave me. I still felt lost and lonely, no one understood, no one could coz I'm odd, it was strong in me, I just thought fuck 'em all, what do they know—boring people?

Being with this family wasn't nice for me, their kids always came first. If they wanted something to eat, they'd just go and get it; if I did that she'd tell me to ask first so to piss her off I'd say "I paid for it". I was jealous of her kids, the cuddles, the bedtime stories, I didn't get it so I'd fuck about every time they got attention. I started to run away more and more. I was 15 now. My care worker came to see me. I really didn't like this lady. Why wouldn't she just piss off out of my life and leave me alone. Her name was Anne Marie. I must say I did fancy her. I used to play games and flirt with her. I'd go red when I saw her and I liked it big time.

Time To Move On

Three

Time to move on again. I was sent to another home for kids a bit older than me. I was glad that they were older. They were into money, drugs and sex and I loved all three. I still didn't like the staff, too nosy, too busy. One good thing was that they stayed in their office a bit more. It was a bigger home, massive house in Sidcup. I met a girl there; she made me feel needed and powerful. We touched, we cuddled, we made love. She made me feel strong and nice with myself. I'd had girlfriends before but this was sure better. She did my washing and ironing; I didn't want to get out of bed in the morning. I didn't feel lost in bed with her, just warm and nice. This went on for a few weeks with her doing everything for me but there was another one I fancied she was older than me, ended up shagging her too. I'd play them off against each other trying to find out which one loved me the most. In the end, after a showdown, they both pissed me off. I told my mate I'd dumped them, as neither was good in bed.

I was nearly 16 and got nicked for armed robbery. It made me feel hard. Me and my mate Victor were tripping out of our nuts, driving around, laughing, having a good time. I loved tripping. We got a puncture in Sydenham High Street. Victor was turning the wheel; I was undoing the nuts and had a wheel brace in my hand. Over the road was a pizza house. I went in, they looked lovely. I ordered the biggest one that they did, I asked the bloke to give me have a closer look at it. When it was cooked he stuck it right under my nose. It startled me, the colours were so bright and the cheese looked like it was moving. I honestly thought that it was coming out of the box to eat me. Crazy, but that's what I thought. I hit the box with the wheel brace the pizza went everywhere. He was not amused and his mate came up to me and said I'd to clean up and pay for it. Though I was scared, I started laughing at him. He went mad and called me everything. I lost it big time and started laying into him. Smashing the wheel brace around his body. His mate joined in, so I hit him too. This time it was his head, body, legs, everywhere. My mate came in then and I put the wheel brace down but I still kept punching. It ended up with me trying to put one of them into one of the big ovens. It's a mystery why I did it. Before we left the shop we emptied the till, £90 something, we were nicked two hours later driving around in the same car. We were taken to Catford nick. The police sure did scare me but I fronted it out. When they interviewed me I gave it the biggun'. My old man always told me, don't tell them anything, the only real evidence they have is what you tell them, I'd never forgotten it. My old care worker came and said, "You're not helping yourself. I went to court three days later. Me and my mate were sent to Feltham. I was real scared. Reality finally hit home about what I'd done. If I hadn't taken that trip, none of it would have happened. They put me in a room with about 20 other kids. I was so frightened

I had to do something in case they started on me, so I started talking to my inmate about the armed robbery, really giving it the big 'un. I really wanted to run and hide but I knew I had to front it out. I started on this young lad rubbing his watch and hitting him. Then I heard my name called "Marsh!" Then a screw came in. I hated him for calling me Marsh. I said "I'm Tony" he laughed and said, "get out of here" he took me into a room with about 20 other screws and they told me to get undressed. I thought they were joking so I laughed. I told them to fuck off. One of the screws said, "Is this your first time in prison?" So he said "just do as we fucking well tell you and you'll be alright. I said, "I'm not taking my clothes off", Rashedy came straight into my head. I couldn't believe they were doing this to me and I refused to comply with them so they tried to help me to take my top off. I went mad and hit one of them. They went mad and took me to a very small room. The only thing in it was a bed; they threw me on it and locked the door. I cried my eyes out that night I didn't even have a fag. I have never felt that alone. The screws came in the following morning and I didn't know if they were going to give me another beating or not, but they asked me how I was. I was in bits really but I said I was all right; I wasn't going to let them win. I was sent to see the prison governor that morning, I'd lost 28 days, no canteen for seven days and seven days down the block on CC, which meant I would see no one. They took my bed out during the day and I was allowed out once a day for some fresh air, I didn't bother and told them to keep it. I felt so unhappy; from there I was put on a wing with 40 other kids. It all seemed so fast after the week I'd spent alone and it made me feel so hard. My new cell mates were nothing but mugs and before long I'd got them doing everything for me. I controlled them and loved it; it made me feel so powerful and yet I was really scared of everything. Even at the gym I had to do more than anyone else or I didn't feel as if I was good enough. Deep down I was scared and lonely and I just wanted to be somewhere else. I didn't want to fight, having to fight in the shower so many times, getting hit by a battery in socks, I'd never give in; if they hit me with their fist I'd go back and cut them. I was hurting them out of fear. If I lost I was scared they wouldn't like me. I always had black eyes, bruises on my head but as long as I was winning it was all that mattered.

Often on visits the screws would try to get my puff off me or my people, it would all kick off. I hated them for it, why did they have to take my puff? I loved it. I was on remand for 11 months. I went to Crown Court Inner London it really scared me. I sat with 15 other kids, some got two years, some eight; some were walking, some were crying, others were laughing. I was praying to God to get me out of there, saying in my mind I'd never do it again. My mate asked me what I was thinking about, I lied and said how much I would like to get the blokes that grassed us up and how I hated them.

They called our names out, I was so scared, scared of their clothes, scared of their wigs and scared of the jury as they filed in and stared me straight in the eye. After three weeks I was found guilty, then a two-week wait followed before sentencing. I was scared but fronted it out and played the hard man once again. While I waited for my sentence I was banged up with a junkie. I didn't like junkies; they were low lifes to me. I was sixteen years old and I knew everything about everything. One weekend I didn't get any puff from my visit so I ended up having a boot. It made me sick but in a nice way, I felt love, I felt warm for the first time, I loved the feeling. I remember saying I'll only do this while I'm in prison. On the next visit from a girlfriend I told her, demanded, in fact that she didn't bring any more puff. Bring me ½ brown, I'll sell the smack and buy puff. It was easier to bring in because it's smaller. I soon learnt the power of smack in prison.

I went back to court and got two years for robbery, two years for the wheel brace and I got one year for smashing the shop up, to run concurrently. I knew I was very lucky, the time flew by, I was selling the smack, I had everyone doing things for me. I had phone cards a good canteen and the best life ever in prison. The screws were always searching my cell, sometimes at three in the morning; they were desperate to find my drugs but they never did.

I was shifted to loads of prisons as my record was so bad for fighting, selling drugs and refusing to comply with anything. I did another extra eight months in prison for bad behaviour and finally got out in July '91. I did try to stop taking smack but I never did. When I got out I already had a half brown a day habit. I'd earned three and a half grand selling drugs inside so I had a start; I was 17 years old and within a month, I was back down the pub on my manor giving it the big 'un. I saw this lovely girl Maria; we slept together and within a week I was with another one; about a month later my mates told me she was pregnant. I went mad and said if she came near me, I'd kick her in the stomach. It wasn't mine and I didn't want it; my mates told me I was out of order but I didn't want a kid.

Toni-Ann

4

I got a new girl, Jo, who was everything I could want, cool, sexy, 21 and rich. I thought I was the man; my mates thought I was lucky to have her and I thought she was lucky to have me. I was selling puff and selling crack, but no one knew about my habit. I was bang on white powder and then got nicked for damaging a house and sent back to prison again. I was still with Jo. I can remember clucking in the police station, I didn't tell anyone. Back in the prison I had a visit with 1/6 of smack, and started selling it again. I was always daydreaming about how I should have done things differently. If only, if only, if only. Within three months of getting out, I got another 12 months. This time the time went by really quickly. I didn't feel so scared, I had everything I needed; I still felt very alone. Yet another birthday came and went inside. More drugs, more using, I'd done about seven months and went for my visit. Sitting at the table was Marie and Jo with a baby girl. I didn't know what to do. I wanted to run but I didn't. Jo said sorry Tony but she's yours. I looked at this beautiful baby and I knew that she was mine. My heart felt something for the first time, she did look like me. I didn't know what to do, walk off or hold her, get my drugs or cry. Marie said her name is Toni-Ann after her dad. Those words were so lovely to hear, I so wanted to cry. Jo saw this and said "I'm going to get some drinks and sweets. Inside I felt like fuck, how could I have such a lovely baby girl. Marie asked if I'd like to hold her. I did and she touched my heart. Jo came back, I could tell by her eyes that this whole thing was hurting her. I kissed my little girl and thanked Marie for giving me such a lovely child. She cried, I wanted to but I knew I couldn't on a visit. I gave Jo the money I'd made selling drugs. I told her to give Marie £100 to buy the baby an outfit. I put the baby in her arms and told her to take good care of her. I got my drugs from Jo ½ of smack, Marie gave me ½ oz of puff so I took that too. She asked me if she could write to me. I said yes even though I knew that Jo didn't like the idea. Toni-Ann was six weeks old that day.

Back on the wing I told myself, "things are different now", how I'd never do another stretch, how I'd give up drugs for good. I loved the fact that I was a dad now. I felt guilty for how I'd treated Marie. Two days later I got a photo of Toni-Ann. She said she could come next week alone without Jo being there. She loved seeing me with the baby and she needed to talk to me. I really wanted that feeling of seeing the baby again so I went to the SO (senior officer) and asked for a special VO. I'd already asked the screws and they'd laughed and said no way. The SO said, "If I grant it will you do me a favour and stop fighting?" I said OK. And I meant it. I also had to think of Jo and the smack. I needed it in there. Marie's VO was granted and she came on the Saturday, Jo came on the Sunday and brought my smack. I told Marie a lie about the drugs; I said I was selling it on the wings but not taking it myself. Jo still kept coming to hand out money and get more smack. I gave her £300 and told her to buy some shoes for my kid. The SO gave me a few VOs every month; I liked him and I think he liked me. I still had the odd fight with those who owed me and wouldn't pay up. I felt powerful in prison. I was selling phone cards for double back. For the next two months

Marie and I saw more of each other; I loved to see her and our little girl so I finished with Jo. Our prison letters got more and more loving, I'd talk about my dreams and she loved it. I did nine months; I was 18 and moved in with her. It was a really nice house in Lewisham, I was waking up every morning clucking but I couldn't tell Marie. It was hard, I'd go to the loo, have a boot and come out feeling full of love for her and Toni-Ann. I loved playing with the baby, it made me feel really nice and so did the smack. I soon noticed that none of my dreams were there with her but I loved Toni-Ann so much.

This went on for about two and a half months, then I was back on remand for beating up the man next door. I got a not guilty after ten months; my prison life was pukka this time. I only felt lonely if I didn't have my gear. Prison letters became my dreams; I did mean it when I said I loved her. I told her I was really sorry for going back to prison. I sold more drugs; I was the man who could get away with everything again. I'd fight with the screws who I thought were too nosey.

I came out at 19 with a 1/6 habit a day. The first night home was nice but I couldn't make love to her so I went out and got some white and made love all night long. She loved it, but to do this I had to use more and more white and the more I used the more I wanted. I did about £5000 in a month. It made me feel so nice in my head and my heart. I told Marie the truth and she said I'd have to stop. I went mad and told her that she didn't understand, it was her and not me, she was the problem and not me. Within two months I was back in a section 18 for GBH; my sister's bloke had started on her; I bashed him up, broke his chin and his arm and smashed his face up. Three policemen had to stop me — I tried to put him under a car; I don't know why I went so out of control.

I really didn't want to go back inside; I pleaded not guilty, lied about my age and gave a false name of "Redford". Aged 20, I was now in Belmarsh. I should have been sent to Feltenham, just as well I wasn't. I was really scared of going there; I'd got sick of the fights with the screws, I thought Belmarsh would be better; it wasn't, they were all bigger than me, had more drugs than me and used bigger weights than me. Even the screws were bigger. I felt really lonely. Marie came to see me with 1/8 of brown, she cried and said "why are you doing this to us?"

I told her to stop everyone was looking at us. I just wanted to stop her from crying. I felt like crying myself, I was scared big time. I made her stop and told her to come the next day. I went back to my cell and got right out of my nut. I liked my cellmate, he sold brown to everyone. He was in for armed robbery; he had a lot of power over the cleaners and other inmates on the wing. We soon became business partners selling loads of drugs. They'd come to me for phone cards and tobacco too; I was main man again although I still felt scared inside. I was away for about seven months and two new lads tried to rob me. They didn't get the drugs, but I was beaten up. I was so scared that if I didn't retaliate I'd keep on getting hit so when we were getting our dinner I grabbed a metal tray and smashed one of them right in the face with it. Using every bit of power that I had. The screws were running all over the place, more towards me than anywhere else. I ran and climbed up the top of the bars and told them I wasn't coming some until "you all fuck off". The screws had been waiting for me to kick off for a long time, so that they could give me a good kicking. I stayed up there for two and a half hours; the whole prison was locked down. The governor said "come down now and we'll let you walk down the block. As soon as I came down the screws rushed me. I went mad, they put me in a body belt and gave me a mad injection which felt ok. One screw was saying "we'll see whose master in here you scum" my whole body was killing me. I ended up getting two years ten months for GBH, section 20; I didn't get with intent to kill, and I thought it was well out of order.

On one of my visits, I was jumped by three screws; I had 1/4 oz of brown. I went into one, jumping over the tables and trying to stick them up my arse. I ended up with another good kicking and another 56 days down the block.

They were desperate to find my drugs. They'd search my cell all hours of the day and night; all they ever found was foil, they hated that but I loved it.

I was always out of my nut; they'd call me junkie. I hated it, I'd say "I'm not a fucking junkie, but your mother and your daughter are junkies". A few months later on an open visit Marie brought me 1/2 oz of brown and a little white. I said "I could marry you" I only meant for bringing me the drugs, within a month the wedding was all arranged. I don't really know how I felt apart from silly. I thought of our prison letter dreams, I knew I didn't really love her, but I thought it would fix me up deep down. I didn't feel right that day in a mad sort of way, but everyone was wishing us luck. I told them that I had to change things now, now that I'm a married man, I was 21 years old.

Toni-Ann looked so lovely in her dress and I loved the feelings she gave me. I loved her smile and I missed her while I was away. I went back to court and got another two years ten months. I was sent to yet another prison—not nice, but I was used to it now. It was a way of life, I didn't feel scared now; I had my drug visits and that was all that mattered to me while I was away.

I was out after about 21 months on a habit of about a gram a day of brown. I was 22. I went home. I walked through the door, it looked cheap and dirty. Within a few days I was selling heroin and white, back with my old mates.

Bad Crimes

5

We decided we had to do something to get some money. We did a bad crime; we had loads of money. I remember I walked in with a black bag, Marie was sitting down; I threw it all up in the air—what an amazing rush I got. Marie and Toni-Ann played with it for hours. I felt so powerful, I went on a nutty one with crack, me and my mates did things that brought us in loads of money.

I ended up buying my first house in Lewisham. One night the police kicked our door in. They found bullets from a

9mm gun so back inside again. I was given 12 months for the first bullet—the rest to run concurrently with the first year so I was very lucky.

My wife told me she was pregnant again; she asked me to stop doing the crime. I said "no, you knew what I was like before you married me" and that was that.

The police tried their best to get my money, but eventually they gave me my bankbooks back and the money that was in the house; I loved it. My son was born in 1994; I was still banged up. I finally got out after doing 12 months. I had to do so much time through piss tests and fighting, my life was madder than ever. I would smoke it all night; I went through so much money, I had to go back out to rob. I started selling heroin and crack. The police were forever trying to nick me. I had a new car; the police hated me and I hated them (still do really). Life went on like this for a few months. I got nicked for drinking and driving—back to Belmarsh for six months. By now I hated my wife and kids. Things were getting worse, I was feeling bad inside. I did four months, me and four of my mates got nicked for murder. It was nothing to do with me. I've got so much shame around this, I was so scared. Top ranking police said that if I didn't play the game and tell them about my mate's part in it, I'd do life. I was shitting myself big time. The girl that got murdered was 19 years old and a friend; I felt so bad inside.

I didn't take part in it, but two of my close mates were found guilty. I was on remand category A for a year, it was in the papers no names though. I was found not guilty; I felt like crying and tears came to my eyes. Her mum and her family hated me and I didn't even do it. I got out and that day I got right out of my nut. I didn't even go home to my wife; I felt like she didn't want me. She said she did, but it didn't feel like it. I sold the house—I didn't like it there anymore. Life went on like this, me doing more and more drugs, spending more and more money 'til it was nearly all gone. Life was shit, I felt shit everyone thought my life was sorted. Nice wife and kids, house, new car but I was lost inside. I felt odd; why should I be like this? Soon I was back inside for something silly; when I came out I had another son, Harry. I knew she was having him, but I wasn't bothered inside. He was one week old when I came out, five weeks went by and on the morning of March 18th at 5am in the morning I found him dead all alone. I was in bits, I went mad and didn't know what to do. I dialled 999, they were talking to me I didn't know what to say. I tried, I really did to bring him back to life. I cut my arms to feel pain, I tried to give him some of my blood to warm him up. The police in their infinite wisdom took it upon themselves to question me and interrogate me just as they did over the murder. Though I knew that I hadn't done anything, I was still scared. Their decision was based on my previous GBH, robbery, violence, firearms, coupled with the fact that I was a junkie. I felt scared by how I was treated so I numbed it in my usual way with drugs, multiple scripts of methadone, amps, Valium amps, Dexedrine and rohiphols from private doctors. I sold our home ended up hating my wife and myself I didn't want to be with her or my kids. We blamed each other, I was scared of losing them but I didn't want to be with them either.

It was 1997, four years ago—I thought it was three but no it was four years. I ended up leaving them. We had £49,000 each—within 6 months I'd smoked every penny of it. Within six months I was back inside again clucking. Found not guilty. I ended up in hospital on a life support machine, tubes coming out of my neck and chest. I was in intensive care, they were saying "they're all trouble" to my named nurse. I could see my bag on the floor, amps, tabs, 4 meth amps, 2 vol amps and 20 dex's, got it bang tight in the chest and gave myself a small heart attack.

I was clean out of my nut. The doctors and nurses were all running around, I was too out of my nut to be scared. The machines were all going off.

My using got worse. I got a blood clot in my leg, nearly lost it. I thought if I'd lost my leg I'd kill myself. In 1998 I was robbing drug dealers and got shot in the top of the leg, once again I might lose my leg. As a result of my drug addiction, I developed lots of illnesses, some of them were life threatening. I suffered five deep vein thrombosis; they developed as a result of injecting a cocktail of drugs that I was addicted to. My drug of choice was "more of anything"—I wanted to run and hide. One of the DVTs was in my arm. I was told that I could lose limbs, another is in my lung. They say I'm lucky to be alive. I could end up with a collapsed lung or brain damage if they went on the move.

In 1999 I went to City Road—I got kicked out for using. I went private and met a lovely lady named Jessie. We were married three weeks later. She had a son Frankie and owned a cab shop. Jessie was really sexy. I told her I didn't want any kids she said she understood and that she had her work and was happy the way things were.

I was both clean and happy and I felt great. We moved to the Isle of Wight for four months, when we came back—I did another job and got more money. We bought a lovely two bed house in Kent. It cost a lot of money. I started selling drugs again and looking after prostitutes. I opened a shop and bought it outright. I had everything I needed and more but still I wasn't happy inside. Then Jessie told me she was pregnant. I hated her from that day. I stayed out even more looking after the working girls night after night. I was still clean, I was there when the baby was born, she was so sweet I felt so proud of her, but not her mum. Her name is Antonia, but I called her Jessie.

I'd started doing NA meetings. I felt very proud of myself. I was on Step 4 of my recovery programme. I didn't want to go home; Jessie and I weren't even sleeping together. Still I ended up back inside, six weeks for a bit of crack they found in my car. I said it was for me (easiest way out) but it was for a working girl. I was still clean at that time.

The End Of The Line

6

I came out of prison and Jessie told me she'd been sleeping with someone else. I felt so lonely inside, I never went home again. My mates sorted my things out. Yet again I spent a hideous amount on drugs, £40,000 in five weeks this time. I went back to City Road again in '01, relapsed again within eight weeks. This time, it broke my heart and didn't help my pain one bit. It didn't allow me to hide away this time, like I'd done for all those years. I did City Road and then came here. I feel for the first time in my life that I belong here.

Finally I'd like to say that beneath my life of crime, I was a young boy craving attention and relief. For the first time in my life I've swallowed my pride and I'm seeking and asking for help to belong. I was always yesterday's nobody or anybody's on the day, but today I'm somebody. I've finally decided to ride this out.

Love Tony

Tony Marsh remains clean 'at least for today'

A Short Cut and Hope

And so, miraculously amongst all this pain and suffering, Tony's story is living proof that miracles can and do happen if you're willing to help them to happen. Tony's saviour now is in the endless work he does to help others. He's found his niche and his purpose, speaking at meetings and conferences, even on TV, in fact anywhere he feels his experiences can make a difference to someone's life. I'd like to thank Tony for allowing me to include him and I'm sure readers will agree that this book would not have been the same if his story hadn't been included. Out of all the stories, Tony's spells hope and that is of paramount importance. And now time to tell you what I have learned from writing this book. It is that we all have to experience pain; for those of us who don't turn to drugs, we deal with it day in day out. There are no quick fixes and without pain, we cannot grow. For some, what ever their reason, drugs are an easy way out but, like everything else in life "the meaning of life" includes that pain to enable us to become decent human beings. All the young people you have read about decided to try to take "a short cut", but have learned by their own suffering that there aren't any short cuts; they only mask layer upon layer of pain and they lose their true selves into the bargain. Inevitably, for each and every one, the day of reckoning arrives and the pain they tried to avoid catches up with them, then they do all of the suffering that drugs have suppressed as the drugs drag each and everyone down to their knees. As you've just read, lives are wrecked, futures are lost, some even pay the ultimate price of death and few of the stronger ones survive to tell their story, like Tony Marsh. Life for all of us is a very precarious journey and far too precious to take the decision to learn the "Addicts Language".

So, I left the best until last because it ends the true case histories on a very positive note. (I'm sure after reading Cases 1–5, readers are feeling somewhat relieved). Tony Marsh is a success story in every sense of the word. Not only has he managed to drag himself out of the mire during the long hard process (Tony's been clean for almost two years now), he has managed to find his true self. As you will see that was not without many failures, lots of soul searching, pain, sheer determination, and guts. His life story holds no secrets, nor does it make any excuses for the things Tony has done. To say that he has come a full circle is an understatement. He told me that the last time he went into rehab, he didn't have a friend in the world. He explained "In a few days time it's my 30th birthday (June 21st) and I'm taking my friends out for a meal, all 35 of them". He went on, "drugs were only one of my addictions. I was also addicted to violence, sex, drink and fags"; they were all parts of Tony Marsh.

Tony's advice to anyone wanting to get clean? firstly join NA. When Tony is sponsoring someone, he never lectures them. He builds up their self-esteem to make them feel worthy. This is because he knows it works. That's exactly what someone did for him. He tries to be patient and understanding and tells them they can phone him anytime 24/7. Tony does not blame his childhood, nor does he have that many regrets (he does have some). Why? Because he says it was his destiny to live the life he did, to emerge as the person he is today. And today he enjoys nothing more than helping others. He has taken the 12 steps of recovery in NA, not once but twice. Tony is quietly spoken and says that the biggest and best lesson he had learned is "Humility" He now spends most of his time helping others and it's very obvious when you see him chairing a meeting that they all hold him in very high esteem. Tony's last comment to me was that we must all remember that with all the will in the world, the desire to get clean must come from the addict.

Judging by the statistics, 1 in 100 get off heroin, which is a testament to Tony Marsh and no matter what your thoughts are when you read his life story, I'm sure you'll agree that to get where he is today took true grit and a lot of will power. I wish him well and feel Tony Marsh has made it.

Quote: "Success comes with being sure in the knowledge that you are at last that person that you were always meant to be"

This is the end of Tony's story.

> Update —Tony Marsh remains clean, at least for today June 12th 2003
>
> 15th October 2003 Tony is in Greece with his girlfriend.

Met up with Tony and Emma last night, it took Tony two hours to get here from Bethnal Green due to a very bad accident. When he arrived he was still wearing his working clothes. Emma looked dreadful, she had more pick marks than ever. Her lower arms were covered, she made us some tea and Tony and I sat at the table. I began to read him parts of her case history. Emma went into the lounge. We heard her crying. Tony spoke to her quietly and gently—she told us that terrible things were happening to her lately. She refused to tell us what they were; Tony said she's in denial.

He spelt it out like this:

Don't

Even

No

I'm

A

Liar

He offered to ring City Road to get her into detox. She declined his offer saying that they won't have a bed. Tony gave her a hug and told her that his mobile would be on 24/7 and with that she disappeared into the night. When I got home I wrote this, which is about how Tony explained it felt in the end. "Like sitting naked in a derelict building with absolutely nothing but his addiction".

After reading the 48, A4 pages that describe very graphically what it was like, I couldn't help thinking it's enough to drive you to drugs. When I compare it with my two sons' upbringing, I can see how lucky they've been. Two good parents, a comfortable home, love and security. Like the majority of kids at the end of the day, he will never know the truth. Did it just become a habit, yes another habit, to say "I Blame Me"?

"No More" describes how Tony's father told him about his mother and also how he broke the news that she'd had two more kids since she walked out on him.

No More

She's got two more kids now
Your sister and your brother
She's asked ta see ye, whadya think?
D'ya wanna see ya mother?
I felt real jealous of her kids
In their safe and cosy home
Eight years old – I'd just entered her head
I felt even more alone

Addicts language

What was the difference between them and me?
These other kids that I hated
Didn't want my mum to touch me
I felt awkward – isolated
How come she'd stayed with them?
She'd left me years before
They played with each other – I played alone
I didn't go no more.

Pride

Red-hot searing anger
My feelings overflow
Desolate, lonely and desperate
For the mother I didn't know
I crave for his attention
My father loosens his belt
I close my eyes and clench my fists
Can't forget how the beatings felt
The silver buckle shines with every thrash, clickety click
I feel small and scared and helpless
He lifts up his boot for a kick
Raining down on my body
Thrashing into my small backside
I bite my lip, and stare at him
You will never destroy my pride.

Many times Tony refers to his mother in his book. How much he needed her. He's never been told why she left in the first place, which simply added to his confusion.

Tomorrow

Tomorrow, she'll come tomorrow
I was six months old when she went
Never got to know the warmth of her arms
I never got used to her scent
Perhaps she just couldn't cope
My young mind tries to fathom it out

It hurts the fact that she left me behind
What on earth is it all about?
I concoct my own mental picture
She's blond slim and quite tall
The truth is in reality
She's probably not like that at all
How I'd love a mum like Billy next door
His life isn't filled with sorrow
Billy is always happy
Perhaps she'll come tomorrow.

Tony got on well with his dad's mate Rashedy. He always had time for him. He often saw him when he was out with his mate and he liked him too. When he began to abuse him physically and sexually he became another man other than his father to hate with a vengeance.

The Bait

He sexually abused me, now I can't let go of his hate
He was my dad's best friend, his loyal and trusted mate
I had such a job sitting down I'd stay in bed the next day
I wasn't prepared for the evil within
He'd always had such a kind way
I hated myself even more
I felt guilty – dirty – disgusting
He took away my soul
Along with it he stole my trusting
He was really fun to be with
He was my dad's best mate
He was out to make a catch
So he used me for the bait

Imagine Being Alone

Imagine a roaring coal fire
In a cosy comfortable room
Relax and it soothes your spirits
Soft and safe like a womb

Addicts language

Imagine a plush warm carpet
Sinking into its sumptuous pile
Next door in striking contrast
Is a home that is daunting and vile
Now
Imagine a derelict building
With no windows, no walls and no doors
Filthy, desolate and empty
Huge gaps in the rickety floors
It reflects the evil drugs stand for
It's cold, it's damp and it's dark
It homes a pathetic existence
It's meagre, it's lonely, it's stark
Now
Imagine that you hold both keys
Avoid drugs choose the welcoming home
If you take them then enter the other
Now
Imagine being alone

Seeking Solace

Seeking solace
Day out and day in
You think you're as strong
As heroin

Seeking solace
You search for a vein
A futile way to ease your pain

Seeking solace
Intravenous affection
Took left and not right
It's the wrong direction

Seeking solace
I chose the wrong key
It's the derelict house

Now I'll never be free

A pitiful existence
Down and out lost
The high price
That seeking solace will cost

I Blame Me

Do I blame the children's homes?
The years that I spent on my Jack?
Do I blame my useless parents
Or the secondhand clothes on my back?
Who can I put the blame on
For all the years that I lost?
Do I blame God?, why didn't he help?
Is he unaware of the cost?
There's nowhere to harbour the blame
They tell me to blame my mother
I search for the answers, I rack my brain
I'm left wondering why I bother
I've given up drugs, at least for today
I seize the moment I'm free
At 30 years old – I face my demons
Let's face the facts – "I blame me"

It Could Be You

How on earth do I find the right words
To conclude a story like this
So many young lives shattered
As they fall into drugs' deep abyss
I search in vain for their reasons
For my own precious sanity's sake
Why, oh why, oh why?
Such a treacherous path to take
Like lemmings they follow each other
The pied piper of death leads the way
To a slow relentless suicide

Yet one more wasted day
Can I ever choose the right words?
They say seek and you will find
But I end up going round in full circles
Depleting my tired mind
Sometimes even words aren't sufficient
They're inadequate so what can I do
The words that keep going round in my head
It must end with "It Could Be You"

Tony Marsh
The Call Of The Wild

Can he finally resist the call of the wild
His tragic fate planned, when he was a child
Beatings, abuse, drunkards and thugs
Who helped pave the road that led him to drugs
NA meetings stand him in stead
When the voice of temptation
Screams out of his head
Cling on to his frayed and well weathered rope
It's fragility mirroring every hope
Can he stay clean and keep away from the dirt
He's aware that it only masked layers of hurt
Can he finally let go of that desolate child?
Or will he respond to the call of the wild

Faking It

Tony Marsh has made it, discarded drugs sharp knife
Overflowing with compassion
No more aching for a life
Yesterday oblivion

Moving on to helping others
Amidst a minefield of lost souls
Relief for all those mothers
Sheer resilience keeps his strength up
He remembers all that pain

He completed his
Apprenticeship a
Scholarship he gained

Moreover he's enlightened
As he knows life's purpose now
Determined and tenacious Tony knows that now
Educating other addicts
Is the path that he must take
Tony Marsh has made it—a human being not a fake

All Over The World

I have found that through the power of words and photos I am able to transport people into my world. The world of a carer to a son with an enduring mental health problem. Using the work included in 'Schizophrenia: A mother's story' and 'Schizophrenia: Through the maze and fighting back', along with family photos, I now train professionals working in mental health. When I say I train, I mean I help them to understand how hard it is and from the feedback that I receive, it works. I now work for The Maudsley Hospital, The Royal Bethlehem and The Institute of Psychiatry which is part of the Thorn Programme. I also work for our local South Essex Partnership Trust. I am hoping to apply this theory to training people about drug addiction. I feel sure that many people have the same narrow views as I had before writing this book and, like mental illness, drug addiction carries its own stigma. If I succeed I will use exactly the same tools as I do with mental health, the power of words and photos to enhance understanding and, much more importantly, they would act as a deterrent. If we could educate people, it would at least be a way forward. I have made the work as powerful as possible. I do apologise to anyone who finds it offensive, but there's no way you can paint a pretty picture of drug addiction. It's repugnant, it's tragic, it's sordid and it's happening all over the world with figures mounting daily.

Preface Two

When Georgina Wakefield asked for my permission to publish my brother's diary, I had very mixed feelings about it. Craig wrote this at a very vulnerable time in his life—a crossroads. He had reached the point where he knew he would die if he didn't conquer his drug addiction. A diary is sacred; an honest account of a person's innermost thoughts and feelings and, unfortunately, this story has no happy ending. I was not able to ask Craig if he would allow this to be read by other people, but after much soul searching I decided it was the right thing to do, because drugs robbed my brother of a life and me of a relationship with a person who I wanted to find the happiness and self worth he had been striving to find for so many years.

I decided that if 'A Life Of Dubious Virtue' could make anyone contemplating taking their first puff on a joint or whatever they are tempted to try, to think long and hard about the tragic consequences, then Craig made that happen, and he would have been proud of the fact.

I have lost my little brother who was young, intelligent and kind with the whole world ahead of him. I tried very hard to make him see that and, because I failed, I have my own demons to live with.

Meeting Georgina may have been fate, but I soon realised that through her own struggles, she now dedicates her time to educate others on mental illness and addictive disorders. In allowing Craig's writings to be published it may, hopefully, assist her in helping others to choose another road.

4

The Final Hit

Road To Recovery

> Craig O'Halloran: This is Craig's real name as requested by his sister
>
> Born: November 9th 1969
>
> Died: September 30th 2000 aged 29 years 10 months.

What you are about to read is written in Craig's own words while in prison. Craig predicts his own death and that he would die before he reached 30. He wasn't far out. Mandy had the unenviable task of identifying Craig three weeks after his death in Islington. He was found in the gutter—not far from a crack-house with the syringe still in place. May he rest in peace.

The Final Hit

On the first page of Craig's diary he's written "Road To Recovery", but this was not meant to be. "The End Of The Road" would have been more appropriate because he met his untimely death as he predicts. At the start of the book, Craig writes about his "illness", his fears, his hopes, his childhood, women, crime and his huge addiction. His diary is a tragic irony and explains very graphically what it felt like to be caught up in the evil clutches of drugs. I have been told by people who knew him that he did try to get help many times, but the waiting lists for rehab are so very long and they all say that, although they understand that this is all of their own doing and it is totally self inflicted, there should be more help than there is. I do feel that many have a dual diagnosis—drug addiction and mental illness. Even in Craig's diary, he talks very early on about his ever racing thoughts and his feelings of utter despair, many of the feelings he relates to are very familiar to me as I have heard my son say them many times. It does make you wonder how many out there try to alleviate the symptoms of mental illness by self medicating with illegal drugs instead of looking for help from professionals. My son suffered for over a year before he would even tell us let alone a GP or a consultant psychiatrist and, in all this time, I have no doubt that he was smoking cannabis, I feel sure the figures are terribly high; it's a very worrying thought isn't it?

When I read the diary I found it to be both shocking and terribly sad. I kept wondering if Craig ever thought that one day it would be part of a book written to try to help deter young people from taking drugs. One thing's for sure, he was very aware of the destruction drugs causes and after reading it I feel 100% sure this would be what Craig would have wanted. His sister tells me that before he got so heavily into drugs, he had the bluest eyes you could ever see. She says that they sparkled and everyone commented on them. But gradually his appearance changed the deeper his addiction became. The one thing that struck me when I first saw Craig's photo was the sadness in his eyes, a mirror of his inner feelings.

Dual Diagnosis

I suppose the biggest lesson I've learned from all of this is that I feel sure that some of these young people were suffering from psychological distress or some type of mental illness as I've said before. I truly believe that my own son self medicated with cannabis and probably other drugs in an attempt to suppress his own feelings following a life threat at the age of fifeen and a half years. It's an enormous question—how many other addicts have taken this form of solace? We will never know; all we do know for sure is that it is the wrong thing to do. And that the only answer is in education, with schools being at the forefront of course; this mountainous problem won't disappear. It will take decades to even make the smallest dent in the problem, but one thing is certain, we can't afford to waste any more time. We have to work tirelessly to try to improve things before our children finally destroy themselves. The Government needs to take the strictest lines with drug dealers; they are let off far too lightly and it's all about money and greed. For those caught up in the evil of drugs already, read this book, digest the words and find the strength that Tony Marsh has found. Think of Tony, think of Craig and decide which role model you want to copy. At the end of the day the only person that can help you is yourself, but you can be encouraged by Tony's story. And Craig's? Well, he is teaching you too, the only difference is that he's not here to tell you his story in person. Nevertheless, his story will be told.

The similarities between Tony Marsh's success story and Craig's tragic end are numerous; the only difference is that Craig was unlucky like many others. He came out of prison and went for the hit that killed him — "the final hit". Tony Marsh managed to find his true self and come to terms with that person, Craig never did. The title he gave this diary, "A Life Of Dubious Virtue", explains his inner turmoil because it's a contradiction in itself, just as he was. As you read it, I'm sure you will end up sad and confused — so many unanswered questions. The one thing you can be sure of is that the evil of drugs has no limits. In the case of Craig O'Halloran, they led him to a slow and relentless suicide. People who knew him say that he would be pleased to have taken part in this book. As a tribute to Craig, I added his title to mine. Who knows, perhaps this was all mapped out. I do find it strange that it should come into my possession. I would like to thank Craig's sister Mandy for allowing me to get his work published and also Emma who gave it to me to use in the first place, neither of us knowing that one day his words would be on the front cover of a book. Although a victim, and although he paid the ultimate price, it seems that his diary was written for a reason and hopefully will do some good, perhaps by bringing some small comfort to those who loved him and, in a strange way, it makes him immortal because his name and the way he describes his own life — "A Life Of Dubious Virtue" — will now live on forever through his own writing. Mandy was told the night before Craig's funeral that his favourite song was "The Runaway Train"; she then played it and broke down—if you read the words you will understand why: see Runaway Train: www.elyrics4u.com/r/runaway_train_soul_asylum.htm

Joint Authors

This poem—Joint Authors—came very late in the book, very recently in fact. Since I've had Craig's diary and photo I've been haunted by both his words and the sadness in his eyes. I've always known that one day the right words would come to me and, as we are co-authors to Addicts Language, I feel very relieved because at 3.15am on Monday 29th September I woke up (as I often do) and there it was. It wasn't until the following day September 30th that I realised that Joint Authors was written the night before the anniversary of his death, September 30th 2000.

Craig and I, two people with so little yet so very much in common, yet destined to be joint authors. So you did make something of yourself Craig, you became an author and a teacher not in this life but in another. Your work will help others and your memory will be kept alive by the power of your words and although you weren't able to save yourself in this life, you are able to at least try to help others save themselves from another life.

Joint Authors

We were destined to be joint authors
As I search your face I sigh
You stare at me defiantly
Why did I have to die?

Your tragic end—and all through drugs
Such futile wasted youth
Your steel blue eyes that sparkled once
Implore me to tell your truth
Your old grey battered diary

Diary: A Life of Dubious Virtue

In which you bare your soul
Inside your words still haunt me
This ever gaping hole

Your tortured mind that rambles on
Invades each fading page
Your relentless search for answers
Your white hot searing rage

For one whole year I've scoured your words
Amongst your poignant writings
Desolation lurks in every line
Tragic, pointless, frightening
Our fated union serves its purpose
For those who share your pain
Your endless search for solace
Will not have been in vain
My gift to you, your gift to addicts
Immortal to prove a point
Stare into his soul, remember Craig
As you re-light your joint

Two Little Boys

Two little boys from similar backgrounds
Both determined to survive
Each searched for years tenaciously
But only one survived

Craig

He was found in the gutter syringe intact
One chilly September morning
Deceased but now a teacher
With a truthful sombre warning
He tells of insecurities
And of what he longed to be
Success came late but he's found his niche in our society
Craig's tragic thoughts rang out that day

Addicts language

Like his life "The Runaway Train"
A mirror for his feelings
The words depict his pain

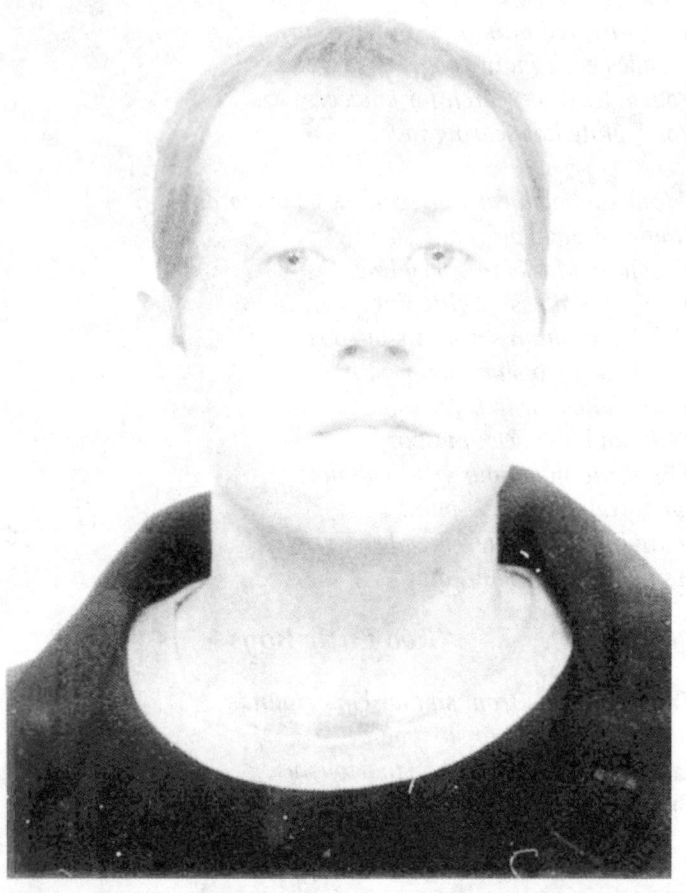

Tony

So what became of the other boy?
The one who did survive
That tortured, lonely, desolate child
Well he's very much alive
Tony? Yes he's a teacher too
And he's doing very well
He lived to fight another day
Transported from his hell
The past is gone his future's bright
At last he found true joys
Parallel lives but diverse paths
In a tale of two little boys

13/7/99; 11.30am; Thursday

First steps

Well here I am again; 'if at first you don't succeed then keep on banging away at it...', got nothing 2 lose and everything 2 gain. To tell you the truth, I'm grateful 2 get another chance... I should be dead or doing life. Today I have the chance 2 live and all the time I was getting stoned and abusing myself, I wasn't alive. I just existed day to day (a terribly, lonely, sad existence at that too: maybe not in the early days, but at the end it was pitiful, but I knew nothing else. My mentality being that I'd made my bed so I had to lie on it and not moan and groan... I honestly thought it was my fate 2 die a lonely, faithless death in a squalid room all devoid of hope. And I was resigned to that; I'd accepted that that was how it'd be.

Come very close to it too; had many brushes with death, days in a coma, but always pulling through against all odds — but these experiences were meaningless 2 me—they didn't penetrate my tunnelled vision quest 4 oblivion. I just felt gutted I was alive really—still in pain and alone (that was and is the key word 4 me—ALONE).

All my life I've lived in my own head, a fantasy world, a dream world, a place of dark thoughts and resentments and obsessions; I never flet a part of, but always apart from? From an early, early age, I felt this way. I never really socialised with other little kids; I spent the majority of my early days stuck in the fantasy world I made up at the time—hours playing on my own...

FRIDAY 14TH JULY

Totally lost the thread of where I was going y/d. Emotional evening—angry—and anger is a really destructive emotion 4 me. Just consumes me totally, eats me up.

Doddy p/c 2 my sister and then I let rip at someone who I care 4 deeply. Where I spent the majority of my years—at least 17—being out of my head, or in prison, or just living in the shadows, the underclass of society—I have trouble relating 2 people, or making sense of my emotions towards other people. The best way I have of explaining is to say I'm emotionally

Diary: A Life of Dubious Virtue

Dyslexic. The only emotions I'm dead clear about are the negative ones; i.e. jealousy, anger, resentment, etc. The only thing I've ever been positive about is the fact I'll die—you're born, you struggle and then you die!—I'm positive about this.

The only person I ever really felt about apart from me was my ol'[mum who's not with us 2day... And that was a twisted and confusing relationship, one that I still ain't too clear about 2day. Yet this girl I know and care about deeply whom I've known 4 many, many years (in fact we go back 2 my childhood ☺) seems2 me 2 not feel the same way or may be not not feel the same way but she's full of her own fears and insecurities about men and the role they should play and relationships (not sure if I'm getting this down clearly) —matters not...I just can't get how I feel about her clear in my mind, not something I'm used to 'cos it's complicated and everything in my life is so uncomplicated and clear cut, but this relationship (if I can call it that) is confusing. I've never felt what I feel 4 anyone else, but does that make it love or mean it'll lust. I've been reckless b4 in the past where she's concerned and so now she doesn't believe a word I say (then again I'm not sure I would ☺).

She's a strange girl, an enigma, full of contradictions but the sound of her voice moves me deep inside, her sigh or her smile just causes chain reactions within me. I see no bad in her at all, to be in her company satisfies me completely if she's mine. What it is about me that desires to own such a creature of perfection and beauty? What would I be like if I did? Is it the feeling of unattainability that attracts me?

Making sense 2 you?

I've been intimate with her, always have been 2 an extent, but I've known her intimately if you get my drift and she's like the powerfullest drug I've taken and I've done them all; and she's given herself to me and confided in me, but my own crazy lifestyle combined with hers has always cancelled out any chance of it going further. She's my island in a storm you see, so what happens when the sea calms and all's well?

Strange times, aye?

All this woolgathering is going nowhere really, just trying to explain how the drugs have left me mentally and emotionally. I don't know how 2 be—to just be! Do you get me? I don't know how 2 be a brother, or an uncle, or a lover. All I know is how 2 feel bitter, how 2 resent and hate, I know how to get angry, but I don't know how 2 love and respect. Probably 'cos at this moment in time, I feel neither of these emotions 2wards myself. So I just hope and pray by staying clean a day at a time, I'll learn to do these things that come naturally 2 th common man who's not afflicted with this self-centred illness of Drug-addiction.

THE ILLNESS   16th July 1999

Okay, fuck it, maybe it's time to get focussed and talk about 'the illness'???

I suffer from this affliction called Drug addiction—basically from the age of 13ish onwards up to the present day, my whole life has centred around using drugs of one sort or another, and mixing with other social misfits who have done the same ('I lived 2 use drugs, and used drugs to live...' (1st of many of the poxy clichés I've come across in my battle to free myself from the chains of addiction.) I'm told I got this illness (like a modern alcoholism) of chemical dependency. And I'll be okay as long as I never pick up a drug or a drink. If I can manage this then my life will be okay and get better. (Tall fucking order 4 someone who used to need a joint 2 get out of bed...) But the moment I pick up, I'm off the rails...and no longer responsible 4 my actions—as I'm an addict who's controlled by the compulsion 2 use! I think this is a cop out really, but it sits OK...☺. I do believe I'm an addict, I think I was an addict from day one—longb4 I picked up drugs. Not sure if it's genetic or nurtured? I hear people—experts and other addicts—that are adamant it's a genetically inherited disorder, and if that's the case, there's proof of the pudding in my family-tree; my dad (in my opinion, though I'm sure he'd beg to differ?) is an alcoholic; his brother and his dad are alcoholics (his brother, Brian was also an addict). My mum was (I think) co-dependant on others to feel happy in herself, my nan and aunt are alcoholics, my cousin has had drug problems—or emotional ones due to her drug intake!!. My nan's dad was an alcoholic, and the majority of her family from her generation have—in my opinion—pretty heavy drunk problems, and the list goes on and on. So it could be genetic! Pretty strong case 4, but at the same time, it could be upbringing; my whole family are dysfunctional in a sense. Hard upbringings, etc.

Maybe some background might help you understand where I'm coming rom. I was born on th 9/11/69 into a single parent family, on the out edge of the London suburbs, in a place called Grays (nr Tilbury Docks), on a council estate (A Labour supporting area). I say a single parent family, but my Dad didn't leave my mum till I was 6 months old. I don't know much about my dad at all; I do know his father was an Irish immigrant and his life was hard. I always had this image of him being a right handy fella, who worked hard with honest sweat and played hard. He was rough, salt of the earth...typical Londoner really.

My mum came from the same sort of background; very tough, Scottish parents, old dockworker her dad was, very tough but very down to earth and honest.

I don't know much about her background either; my grandad's dead and my nan won't talk about the past, so all I can gather is it wasn't a bed of roses—from what I can glean, it was a hand 2 mouth existence for all on the breadline in those days—and our upbringing was no different.

As I write this, I'm sitting in a prison cell on my 8th sentence 4 drug-related crime. I've spent 7 yrs almost out of the last 10 yrs behind bars...I grew up being told this would be where I'd end up and I think subconsciously I strove to prove everyone right. I'm now almost 30. I have no children to carry on my name or bloodline; I have nowhere to live, no money put aside, no respect 4 others, no future as such, no qualifications, a criminal record 4 dishonesty a mile long, a stinking attitude towards society and life, and I harbour a bitterness within my heart that's almost impossible to put into words. Where did it all go wrong? When was the decision made to follow the path I did? Why did I sacrifice all the things I just mentioned 4 chemicals, 'cos this is what I've done.

It's as though by the age of 16 or 17 I'd given up completely on life and turned to the oblivion from all feelings that only chemicals can give. Yet I'm not sure when the turning point came. My mum had 3 kids, my half sister Lorraine who was adopted by my Nan and Pop as she was illegitimate, my full sister Amanda and finally me. The blue-eyed boy who could do no wrong—not at first anyway.

I think I was her (my mum) replacement 4 my dad who I know she loved very much and vice versa, as she never really loved another. I was my Dad, yet I could be moulded to how she wanted. Love was something I never wanted 4 in the early days. I was smothered in it by all the women in the family, to the extent of almost suffocating from it later on in life and doing everything in my power to smash my way out from the Prison of conditional love and emotional blackmail I felt I was in. And then doing everything in my power to destroy all healthy relationships I had, and everything I could to to live a loveless life once having escaped. This is all very confusing 4 me to recall 4 some reason. I feel I'm betraying my mum's memory, but its me being as honest as I need to be 2day 2 stay clean. She didn't know no better. She done her best 4 me, she was just a product of her upbringing as were her parents and so on and so forth...That's why I believe more in the Nurture arguements rather than the Nature.

My full sister never had it so good at all. She suffered at the hands of our mother greatly. Mum tortured her mentally and physically right up to her lying in her death bed. I get very emotional thinking of the life she had compared to me at the hands of mum. I feel immense sadness and guilt still to this day when I look into the eyes of my sister. I see pain, loneliness and sadness to a depth I could never comprehend, but she strove to succeed and succeed she did. She's now an independent business woman that's comfortable in life. But still I look in her eyes and I see they are haunted by the memory of my mum's ghost. Maybe it's me that's haunted by these memories and all I see is a reflection of my own eyes?

I've been estranged from my sister for many years due to my drug problems. She, like the rest of my family were (and still are to an extent—although 2day there is a degree of understanding) rightly reviled by my drug addled behaviour. But to her credit, she found me a squat recently and gave me the chance of redeeming myself and offered me the love and support to do it (but that's another chapter....)

Only my mum will ever know why she was so resentful and full of the twisted bitterness she felt 2wards my sister. I think it stems from the fact her 1st child was snatched from her arms at the birth by her parents and told to call her her sister and never to tell anyone otherwise—I honestly think this had a profound effect on my mother. Forever twisting her mind and feelings towards her next child who was also a girl. But like I say, I'll never know. It's something my mum took to her grave.

Is any of this relevant? I don't know, but it's all part of my story, so it needs to be told in its entirety. I'm afraid you'll just have 2 get comfortable. My mum was so full of love at times, but she could be a tyrant. We were terrified of her the majority of the time. At 1st the abuse was mainly 4 Mandy while I got the love, but as soon as I come of an age where I begin thinking 4 myself, it came my way too, just not as often or intensely—at first. Yet later on I suffered just as much at her hands.

She was a very controlling, dominant woman who demanded obedience and woe betide the one that didn't give her it...

19/7/99: Monday morning aboard the floating prison...

What can I tell you? Not a lot I suppose, not much happens here; I just exist in my own head mainly...I stay away from all the bollocks so my reality in here is pretty straight 4ward and boring (but that's a state of mind).

2day I live quite peacefully and honestly...I'm not out 2 tet what I can, I don't prey on the weak, I do what I say, and I say what I mean. I don't lie 2day, there's no need 4 it...I keep myself 2 myself and don't bother anybody, but still, I'll protect my own space if need be... But that's the bonus of staying out the drug scene, no-one really notices you. I got this invisible existence off to a tee. There's a part of me that yearns to be in amongst it all, but there's a bigger part that knows where it'll lead me so I have 2 hold onto the painful memories of where my addiction took me; you see the addiction is not just about taking drugs, it#s lifestyle attitude, state of mind. The whole thing.

Addicts language

It's been a way of life 4 me and to change it's got to be a complete transformation. I need 2 go the whole hog... I was hooked into the danger of it all, just as much as the chemical rush. And this is something I must stay aware of...if I 4get then 4 me it's the 1st steps on a slippery slope. Drugs 4 me 2day equal incarceration. 'Prisons, institutions and death'.

I can't use successfully; I've tried time and time again but to no avail. I've swapped and changed drugs, areas, friends, tried religion, done various rehabs, done lengthy prison sentences (I've been given since the age of sixteen, seven sentences, plus remand time) and nothing changed. This is because all these things I looked at were outside of myself and 2day I know it's me that's the problem, not the drugs or anything else.

For me 2 live such a decadent and faithless existence, an existence devoid of hope, love and meaningful relationships, means a lifetime devoted 2 pain, regret and bitterness. By doing this, I've denied myself the opportunity 2 experience life in its true form, 2 experience other people, 2 taste the essence of love, 2 experience the mantle of self-responsibility. I'm bigger than this; I'm made of sturdier stuff. I'm not your average joe, there's more to me. I need fulfilling on a higher plane you see and I won't rest till fulfilment is reached. I've forever looked outside of myself 4 spiritual fulfilment and all along it's been within me, and it's been there all along patiently waiting 2 be let free...

I read a lot; I'm forever searching you see, but just 'cos I read and like what I read, that doesn't make it gospel. Everyone has their own truth and their own reality, and I'm halfway 2 finding mine. It's been a long, hard path and, at times, I thought I'd never make it, but things are becoming clear 2 me.

Here's some Shamaniac writings I've been reading that to me are pretty amazing and simple at the same time. Like I said b4, just 'cos they make sense 2 me, that don't make them Gospel and 2 you they might be just waffle. But they are signposts that give me directions on my path 2 find my truth and my reality.

Diary: A Life of Dubious Virtue

The first bit of writing is by an Indian called Shadow who lived in the mountains alone and tended sheep:

"We experience our greatest fears and our deepest pain, our sorrow, when we must leave our beautiful earth, mother life. So, wanderer, why is it that many humans will throw away their lives to prove the ridiculous? Why do people prefer their pretense instead of the joy of life's challenges? Who is family when we never know them?
Does language make a race, or does belief make a race?

You should ask these questions!"

"Appreciation of life is the most honorable of all the tools of the mind. Do you know this tool? The powerful know this tool intimately. Appreciation and knowledge are the most powerful tools given to humans in any lifetime. Appreciation of life is the tool of attainment..."

"You can find your life, but only when you see the truth of your circumstances and the challenges that exist in your time. Search for the person you are, not the person you wish you were!
 Confront your own world of mind. What is it that exists in your world? Who are you in your world—the slave or the commander?"

"Do you know what arrogant men fear? They fear they can never possess the powerful or the beautiful. What they do is substitute their fear for their arrogance and try to buy their lives. Life will never be their prostitute; they cannot buy their lives..."

"Life is precious; it is the most profound of all experiences known in creation. Life is sacred and ever-present because life is prescience. To try and escape the rigors and rewards of mother life is to escape existence..."

Addicts language

"Life is our great teacher. The most profound reason for the existence of life is that each person has the opportunity to experience life and to learn self-responsibility. Who we are and how we live our lives is our great question and wondrous answer. Self-teaching is one of the most profound reasons that humans live. When we teach the self, we recognise the spirit of the spirit of mother life and learn to respect the energies that birthed us all."

"So, earth wanderer, welcome to life."

Bits go over my head, but the majority leaves me speechless. It's so simple really. cherish your life and don't waste a single second. Appreciate it all 'cos it's a precious gift. The pain as well as the joy.

Anyone reading this would probably think I'm off it, but fuck them; it ain't 4 no-one but me, not meant 4 fucking debate no way at all; and anyway I am off it compared 2 general joe public—like being off it gives me a flavour and keeps me occupied. ☺ I hear, read and see things all the time that I like, words are wicked mate and I wish I had the power 2 express myself as powerfully as the man I just wrote about. I'd kill 4 this gift. I try and that's all I can do.

> Well, it's got nothing 2 do with anything that is real
> You just believe in it and it's true...
> You can soothe like an angel or sigh like a saint
> You can dream it and see it through
> You will live 2 see a sea of lights
> Sparkling on the face of a pearl...
> Climb your own peak, find a new streak,
> Get yourself along with the world
> Now you been building 4 yourself a cool place in the sand
> Your thinking that its mighty fine
> You got dust in your eyeballs, you got mud in your mouth
> But its your head, it ain't mine...
> I gotta madman of my own 2 contend with
> cursing in the cave of my skull...

Diary: A Life of Dubious Virtue

Turn the other cheek, find a new streak
And get yourself along with the world
But I heard a rumour of a golden age
somewhere back along the line...
Maybe I dreamed it in a whisper or heard it in a spell
It was something 2 do with the sign of the times...
But the only thing that I remember is a summer like a pretty girl
Who shimmers and shines, moving in time,
Shaking 2 the beat of hearts and the world
Shaking 2 the beat of the world.
  (need reference - who wrote this and when)

I think I feel too much, not don't feel anything like I always thought. I overload on feelings. I'm so sensitive (and I don't mean that in the soft sense) 2 things, people and situations around me. Its like I'm so highly tuned that I just take on every vibe in my vicinity. I read into every little thing I see or feel or read. I can even pick up on people's thoughts and feelings in letters, even when not put in them. It's what ain't said and the tone of what is said...Yeah, I think that's my cross 2 bear, that I feel too much and too deeply. And I'm no good at feelings, I've run from them 4 so long you see. I've got my reasons but still that's no excuse 2 keep running, I see that now. I want to experience every feeling fully. It's OK to feel and feel empathy 4 people....it's ok to be sensitive.

I'll hear lyrics sung and feel deeply and connect with the singer and comprehend totally where he's coming from and relate it to my own life. Is this a good thing or not? I know not; what I do know is I'm going 2 learn to live with myself, my feelings, my fears and experience what life has 2 throw at me. No more chemical avoidance. Time 2 be the man I know I can be. Who is strong, dependable, honest, disciplined, yet compassionate, caring and loving. I got the capacity 2 be all these things. No doubts no more! I'm decided on this. If it all fails, the drugs and oblivion is always there waiting 4 me 2 fall back on. I want 2 blossom and grow into the man I'm well and truly capable of being. It's important 2 me....

Addicts language

OK, enough crap 4 2day boy; it's been a good day 4 me still. Enlightening...

Here's some more writings from a medicine woman of the Indian Nation — Estmicha (EST-MEE-CHA):

"Those who love and care for the self will, one day, learn to know the self. How will you find yourself?

Human suffering, ignorance, joys, enlightenment—all of our wondrous life journey is 4 me life herself. I see all this when I smoke my pipe. I have seen the results of 2 world wars. Humanity strides along a highway of skulls it calls progress because, they say, out of war was born the new mechanised technology. I quake inside, like the doe that has lost her fawn, when she hears the thunder held in the hands of humans.

I believe that beauty is so much here on earth; it overwhelms the minds of the people. I think humanity is afraid to live in beauty. I think that humanity is afraid of the challenge of living in beauty.

The pipe is so simple. The pipe is so very subtle. The pipe says that we can have cities with wide avenues of flowers and trees. The pipe says that we don't need to walk along highway of skulls. The pipe says that each of us is our own authority in life, and that profound truth makes everyone of us responsible for our lives. Those who truly respect the pipe must also respect the sacred self that they are. How very delicate the self is! How very fleeting our lives are" (I wouldn't mind a few of these fucking pipes at the moment ☺). "Life is not easy, but life is not nearly so hard when we honor the self."

"Most people never get angry enough to do anything about their lives. They are satisfied just naming the weakness and being its victim. Such people miss the beauty of life. For beauty is perfectness and balance. Yet how many humans really know beauty? Beauty is strength and she is challenge. How many people know strength and challenge."

Diary: A Life of Dubious Virtue

"Most people view beauty as a weakness. You must learn that being the toughest guy in town is a weakness. Having a desire 4 money is a weakness. Another weakness many humans suffer from is their enjoyment in pointing out other people's weaknesses.

We are taught to believe that weakness is given in a person's life and that nothing can be done about it. Weakness i like a disease that's incurable...
 To be in "love" is viewed as a weakness, not a strength. Love and life are the human experience we know as existence. Yet how many people know that love means sharing?
 Love is the visible form of sacred life. She is beauty. Our experience of knowing life is knowing love...love is the highest of expressions and feelings know th humans.
 Love is life herself."

And something everyone needs 2 experience without conditions I think. Any love I've ever felt has been conditional.

Bad few hours earlier on. The power of my loneliness overwhelms me at times. It's like I got this hole inside of me that swallows me whole at times. Just sort of sneaks up on me... The majority of the time, I keep my loneliness and pain locked away as the power of it scares me. Just weighs me down. I feel totally defeated and just want to die really. It's a solid lump in my bely; it burns me up, becoming a physical thing, almost tangible. I can taste it, feel it even.

It's hard work here, I hardly speak 2 anyone. I speak but I don't connect. Prison starves you of spiritual connections...connections that feed your sould. Ones that matter and make your heart sing. Get my drift?

In here, I'm just totally isolated. There's only one person I really want to be around ☹ and it ain't happening... I try not 2 think about her much. Confuses me. She's a strange creature but that's the attraction 4 me. I never knew a girl like it . Best friend I ever had, best sex I've had and I've not been starved in that area...☹☺ Just something about the bird...But I put her as far from my heart as possible as it's got no future. We are just meant 2 be pals. God give her me 2 keep me on the straight and narrow...This sentence has hurt me in that respect. I think of her and I feel blue ☹ No wonder she's reluctant to get involved emotionally. She's no fool.

She makes my heart sing though ☺ I got no doubts of that. (better leave it there... I'm blue enough).

20/7/99

Tuesday morning, still feel blue, having trouble shaking the feeling of being an island. This feeling is always with me, but don't normally show through; I'm good at being 'ok' but occasionally it just drowns me and it takes a few days 2 pull out of it. Why am I such a freak, why do I feel so deeply when all around me just plod on oblivious? Does my head in.

Feel like getting high...

Hope I get a letter but I know I won't... Even if I do I got a bad feeling about it. Feels ominous. Last night I was awake till about just gone 2 —thinking sick thoughts again. My mind seems 2 have a mind of it's own. I got no control over it when it gets going on one — all I can do is hold it down and ride it out till the sick fucking fantasies run their course.

I heard keys outside my cell about 1.30 and this bad feeling came over me; had the vision of another death being there and I'm here. Went back 2 my ol' mum... Bad thoughts but that's all they are; I'm not a well person in my mind at times. What I think isn't necessarily reality. I have 2 really hold on 2 that one and work out what is reality. Not the sharpest tool in the shed you see...

I'll get better, I know that, just a passing phase—my black period. As long as I don't pick up, things will improve. I'll 'recover' ☺ I have 2 smile when I say that, I just think of J.....☺

I have got faith this time....

I just put in 4 a HIV test ☹ I got a bad feeling. I pray I'm wrong 4 a whole bunch of reasons—not so much 4 my sake ☹ I've been battling with it 4 a while now. Shall I bother? Sha'n't I? Is it worth knowing? It's the responsible thing 2 do. My future hinges on it... Fucking worried really. I think this is what the moods all about.

It doesn't just affect me does it? And I can't talk about it. I just think my luck has run out...This prophecy I've had 4 years about being dead by 30. Well, it all hinges on this...I need 2 know.

What would I do if it was positive? Big fucking question? I'm not hanging around 2 die slowly, put it that way. Maybe a cop out but it's how I'd deal withit.

Would I have the courage 2 face it? I really don't think so, I'm not the corageous type you see, I run from everything; it's my pattern I'm afraid ☺ Wish I was different but I'm not; I am what I am.

Would I have the courage 2 take the easy way out? Again I don't know! I love fucking life so much it hurts. I'm scared stiff of dying at this moment in time. Maybe that's because, finally, I've got a taste of my own mortality.

It's only been the last month that the irresponsible way I was using in them last weeks has hit me. You don't think at the time...

What about pem ☹ Does my fucking head in thinking about it. If she wasn't in the equation I wouldn't want to know. But I put her in danger too, haven't I? So I got 2 know... This could shatter only sacred relationship I have...

And that wounds me...

But it's all what ifs at the moment; let's get it over and done with and take it from there...

21/7/99: 8.00am

Feel right as rain again; jumped up this morning, banged on som R&Bs & whacked it up (FUCK HIM ☺) Tidied up; can't quite get the hang of this housework☺. Sorted myself out and now I'm sitting thinking...The clouds passed, got views on it, just starved of connection with people I desire 2 connect with. I got a feeling I'll get a letter 2day that'll bring me down again...fucking hope not...

Got a few things 2 say but its brekkie now so I'll leave it 4 10 minutes.

Addicts language

Just feels a relief 2 be in the right frame of mind again... When I get like I was, I get angry at everyone and everything. Close 2 blowing all the time but I just hold it down or put on a face of indifference and calm, but all the turmoil and anger's still there. Just building up 4 the big one ☺ Only just sort of seeing how much of an angry man I am... fucking hard work... I don't know how my people still bear with me... I must wear their patience thin☺!

It's mad really, 'cos I was laying in my pit last night (alone☹) and my head was doing its usual wandering routine, and all of a sudden I had this vision of me getting a place in Somerset. Went through all the motions of decorating it and that, had it all done out in Native American style, so I built this coconut bong and only would smoke sensy through it (AS IF ☺), which I will grow in my attic and everything will be peaceful and content, and then I sort of come too and laughed— that's a prime example of fucking denial ☺ major case? I was smiling 4 ages..."If only I could have a little place and my bong with a free supply of weed" then my life would be sweet—I mean, what a load of bollocks aye ☺ .

Had some good little visions 4 the future though. It's funny how they all contain J......☺ I should be prepared 2 have 2 do all the stuff I gotta do on my todd though. I'm just looking 4ward 2 doing things with her, that's all...

I want 2 take the girls 2 Glastonbury.

23/7/99—Thursday

Had loads of stuff come up in my nut the last couple of days, but the thoughts come so fucking fast and furious that I have trouble keeping tabs on them. I mean 2 write them down later but can't seem 2 translate the thoughts and feelings into words on paper...You see I know my head's pretty mad at times, so I try 2 filter out the insanity, the little voice that tells me sick things, that tells me not to trust no-one I mean no-one, not J....., not even M...... I just don't trust no-one and it's sad really.

With J....., I don't believe a word she tells me basically, and maybe that's a reflection on me (she'd definitely agree on that point). With M....., I think she just feels duty-bound.....but deep down she doesn't like me. Maybe she'd like to, but in her eyes I'm

Diary: A Life of Dubious Virtue

a div. Same goes for P... with that one. She just means well, wants to gee me up so she shines 4 me. But deep down these people underestimate me. Don't <u>really</u> know what I'm about, never plumbed my depths (fucking hell! Where'd that one come from.) Seriously though, they don't know <u>me</u> _ the real me, 'cos not even I know me. Anytime I show through, no-one who matters to me has glimpsed it. I got all those different personas 4 different people, you see, and they subconsciously slip into place as I interact. I'm a social chameleon in that respect....It's comfortable 4 me 2 play the role that's been built 4 me I suppose. I slip in that way and fit. I don't know really, that's something I got 2 think on at a later date.

I'm resentful and angry at the moment...When I handed myself in, I came in with all the promises that I'd get all the mail in the world, visits..blah...blah...blah..., and I get nothing really. Novelty soon wears off. I feel hurt and rejected really – especially by J......

Can't even get some music 2gether. I ain't really pestered no-one 4 nothing. I think they could be more supportive man, but they think I'm OK, I'm hardened 2 it, but it's balls. I'm more insecure than I've ever been.

I gotta make sense of this relationship with J........

I can't believe it's almost 7 yrs ago when I first fucked her. She's an amazing girl, I'm bewitched by her.... It ain't the same in return though....So I got 2 be careful, she's trouble (and I don't care) and too much 4 me. I slept with a lot of women but no-one's touched me like that girl and the fact it's one way freaks me. She can't give me what I want and I fear it's the same in reverse... The foundations 4 a solid relationship are there, best friends (or am I deluding myself there?) and fucking, blinding sex. She's the horniest bird I met. I just have 2 think of her and I get hard. But it takes a little more...

I come in on a high from that girl and the come down was fucking terrible. So much is unsaid and I hate unsaid things. I need things 2 be in the open and all clear. Is it just a casual thing? Has it got future? Can I trust her with my emotions? Does she want what I want?

Bottom line is I want more than casual.

Addicts language

All this is just prison bollocks, that's why I don't say shit 2 no-one. Glad I can get it out my nut though.

The fact no-one writes don't help though. I'm on my todd here, and that's a fact. Everyone's just too busy 2 be really bothered. And that's OK – fact of life. Just a hard fact 2 swallow.

Don't see why it should be, be alone 4 many years. Just had this fantasy when I come in it was all gonna be different this time... but nothing's changed. Talk's cheap, that's why I'm giving up with it all. Just focused on staying clean and bettering myself. I'm gonna allow myself 2 be the the man I'm capable of being. Had it with chemicals. I'm tempted 2 write but fuck them. I don't need no-one really, I can do this alone, I <u>will</u> be OK. Just hurts. But it'll pass... s'only a fucking feeling mate.

About 2 hrs or so after – not been doing much, nothing 2 do except think or take gear....options are pretty limited really. I keep myself busy most of the time, but there' periods when I'm left 2 my own devices when I just sink..There's times when I think this fucking addiction is just too powerful 4 me and my destiny is 2 die with a needle in my arm, alone, in a dirty hove....You reap what you sow.

It's bollocks though, I have 2 really stand firm with that though, it's my dark side trying 2 trip me up...instilling doubts, injecting fear, and sowing negativity. There's a big part of me that thinks I don't deserve 2 live, 2 love, and receive love, 2 respect and receive respect, that part of me tries 2 condemn myself 2 living in a personal hell, sentencing myself 2 a lifetime of pain, anger and bitterness. Lately, I feel like getting high all the time, and it's 'cos ok all this turmoil I got going on. I fight it everyday. My demons plague me constantly...And its hard, I got 2 be honest about it – I'm really struggling. If heroin was in front of me now, I'd take it... I fucking hate the stuff, it's ruined me completely, brought me 2 my knees, ripped my family from me, literally shattered my life yet I still yearn 4 it's warm embrace, 2 soothe the pain I feel. I despise myself so how can anyone else like me or love me – Why?

Why not just be upfront and tell me what I fear? You see, this is the extent of my madness, at times the insanity just overwhelms me. It takes all my resolve 2 get to last bang up with out scoring, then I'm safe. I go 2 bed and pray 2morrow it leaves me alone, and 9 x's out 10 it does, although this little bout has been on me 4 days now. I'm gonna try and write 2 my sister and see if I can convey how I feel 2 her...

Well that's done but I'm not sure how I feel about it. Do I feel better now I've wrote it but do I send it? We'll see in the morning how I feel

Wish I weren't such a nutter. Life would be so simple.

I CAN BEAT THIS!!!

DON'T GIVE A FUCK HOW POWERFUL IT IS!

I deserve a life....

23/7/99

Feel fucking bundles better, not a bad start 2 the day, glad 2 be alive... Think the letter's purged me. Gets it out the system – wrote P...too. I'm not sending them though. Just needed 2 get shit out...

The sun's shining and I'm just relieved. Wonder if I'll get mail, I'm torn in that respect – part of me wants 2 hear off her but at the same time it's hard work, just kick start my nut again – and it's took nearly 7 days 2 settle again....

Life'd be so much easier if they all just wrote me off....It's no wonder I struggle with life without drugs – I been getting out of my head since I was 13.

I remember the 1st time I started getting high – I'd been sent away 2 a school – a private school funded by the Council – and I just couldn't work out what I'd done, felt abandoned really, (the 1st time I went away I was 8) so my institutional career started at an early age. I've got really good vivid memories of the second school I went to... the 1st was painful and lonely, I honestly thought it was something I'd done. Why wasn't I wanted around home? Shit happened at this place and I just thought I was bad and that was why it was happening. What other reason was an 8 yr old doing in a home miles away from home when he had a family that was more than capable of having him home? This had a deep psychological effect on me, no doubt about it... I done everything possible 2 get awy. I was eventually expelled 4

Addicts language

fighting at the age of 10. Unfortunately, the kid we beat up was a copper's son and the dad tried hard 2 have me taken 2 court 4 it. So a compromise was reached and I was sent home in disgrace and I was buzzing – took me 2 years 2 get out of that hell.

So I came home 2 all my mates and went to a local school, and was back where I belonged with my family...I was clever, always have had a sharp brain and been quick 2 learn. So I done well at school 4 my last year at primary and life was ok on all fronts 4 the 1st time in a few years. I had all my pals from the old days... life was good. My memories of this year I spent at home art the best in my life. I was a tearaway but harmless... Then came the summer break and we were all prepared 2 go to camp 2gether. I honestly believe if this is where I'd gone from day 1 life would have been very different 4 me. But I was dropped with the Bombshell I was being sent away again...

I was devastated, didn't want 2 go... But I had no choice, 'it's 4 the best' I was told so off I was packed, alone and abandoned again. 'What had I done that was so bad?' I just couldn't work it out at all...

It was an all boys school, just 250 – Elmwood Private Boarding School at Fifield, Chipping Ongar, Brentwood. Very posh school, quite upmarket. The truth is I deserved 2 be there. I was intelligent and was being given the chance 2 get a real education. My truth was I was in another home, I'd been sent to prison... So the 1st year was very sad and very lonely, very isolated and to this day them feelings of loneliness and isolation have never left me. I wasn't accepted there, I wasn't posh, I was a charity kid, single parent family and hadn't earnt the right 2 be there... There was a few of us 'charity kids' there and it didn't take long 4 us 2 just stick 2gether.

I did excel there. I loved it after a while, I was top in English, maths, French, and I done well in all my studies. It was a way 2 avoid things 4 me – an escape from reality.

I came home every month and begged 2 be allowed 2 stay home, but No – 'It's 4 the best' I was told. In other words, I wasn't really wanted my head decided...After a while I stopped the tears and toughened up. I fought back when I needed to with the snobs, I was always fighting – don't know why, 'cos I couldn't fight, the thought of it scared the life out of me but I had to keep people away. I was smoking by now, climbing out my window in the dead of night and walking across the fields and through the woods exploring. I used 2 run away regularly but was always caught in the next town or train station and returned. (My hitch-hiking and travelling career started early, aye?)

I remember my 1st real buzz. We would bend down and breathe fast – in out, in out, and so on 4 about a minute till you was dizzy and then you'd stand up fast and some one would press your chest in a bear hug till you passed out and lay on the floor twitching. Biggest head rush you could imagine... Mental really, crazy and dangerous but I couldn't get enough of it. I'd come around and do it again and again.

My thieving and creeping career took off soon after my midnight explorations – I'd see open windows and do S A S manoeuvres, really getting off on the adrenalin. Burgled the tuck shop numerous times, through the window, through the door, through the walls, through the fucking roof. Only thing we never done is build a bleeding tunnel.

End result of this nutty progression was I got caught and suspended. Did I fucking get it boy, I couldn't sit 4 days, my arse got whopped... By now I was having the time of my life. All thoughts of leaving had gone... Biggest adventure of my life; I was wise 2 the world now and knew the score...

More fights, more midnight expeditions, studies suffering, and finally middle of the 3rd year I was asked 2 leave. Gutted I was, went home in disgrace again, now I'd lived up 2 what I thought I was bad...

Back home and bunged into comp, all out of sync with all my ol' pals totally, the whole game had took a slant 4 the worse.

My mum was never settled, we didn't stay in a house for more than 2 or 3 years sometimes even less. I got the name gypo. We had no money as such a very hand 2 mouth existence and it rankled me... I was ashamed...

I just went all out 4 acceptance, I'd do anything 2 prove I was one of the boys, anything at all. I was crazy but I weren't really, I was scared of my own shadow, scared of not being accepted and being rejected. I just wanted 2 belong but I never did; if anything, my behaviour ostracised myself more.

"In the desert
I saw a creature, naked, bestial
Who, squatting upon the ground,
Held his heart in his hands
And ate of it.
I said, 'Is it good, Friend?'
'It is bitter, bitter,' he answered
'But I like it
Because it is bitter
And because it is my heart'".

Stephen Crane (Black Riders III)

24/7/99 Saturday

Nothing much 2 report from the bowels of the system – uneventful day, no mail, funny ol' turnout but fuck it. Don't know why I expect different. S'always been the same. You reap what you sow... So I got a pretty sad harvest coming my way...

This tin can is sweltering, being baked and 'cos every cunt is using the air-conditioning, its just overworked and only dribbling out; hard work with 2 in a cell – no air, just have to lay with a wet towel, keep cool... Not been a bad day 4 me, just choked on the mail front, but it's my front 4 believing people – I've done all I can, fuck them, just time 2 go my own way again. Only setting myself up anyway...Big Boy!!!

The sun was blinding 2day, my tan's come on a treat, only out there in it 4 an hour playing chess. Do really find it hard 2 focus at the moment, my mind is all over the place, busy, busy, busy. This fucking sobriety is a headache mate but I can handle it. Getting sharper all the time.

Just been told I'm not my normal self; hardly surprising really. Wouldn't say I'm miserable, just reflective and thoughtful. Weighing up my life and the relationships in it. Needs a review really. So all in all, I'd say I'm just having a good look at things from every angle – end result inevitably a bluish mood... That's about all from me 4 2day, I'm tired, hot and sweaty so I'm gonna sign off and have a shower, read some Wilbur Smith, listen 2 a bit of music and sleep. Saturday night and I'm 2 my bed alone at fucking 11pm – bitter 2 swallow. Consequences of self sbuse. Just got to take it all in my stride...

25/7.99 Sunday Night 7.30 pm

Wrote 2 my big sis at last – posted b4 I changed my mind yet again... She still got the carefully edited version Spineless c*** aye?

I refuse 2 allow myself 2 write P.... I'm just waiting 2 see whats what...

Fuck her, I'm going on like a mug mate, so what if I like her, the fanny every where out there, far less complicated 2...

S'only the Jail Vibe that does me...

Tuesday 27/7/99;

> Well, feel ok as it goes, bit blue but that's just the thought of another 7 moon in here, pulling my prick twice a day – now I'm clean I'm horny as fuck; mush... Typical aye...
> Gonna do a meeting 2night, different faces and that. Wish I could say I'd cracked it with the AA and that but it'd be bullshit. Keeps me occupied in here that's all. I'm gonn still get charged and as drunk as possible and as laid as often as I can... Not quite ready 4 Spartan existence yet, still got things 2 run...
> I'm stronger than I think, have flashes of it now and again, but it's coming mate – longer I'm off the gear, it'll get better. Pucka letter y/d off my sexy cuz. She's as good as gold really. Scorpion through and through...

Wednesday 28th

Feeling good – still got this virus bollocks on my brain – having the tests 2morrow, take 2 week 4 the sesults at the outsides, then I know either way don't I?

But like I say, on the whole I feel sweet – seems 2 me the longer it is getting no news off those who 'matter' the more relaxed and easier I feel. Strange state of emotional affairs really. Don't think I'm working 2day, all dressed and waiting but it's gone 9 and I've heard nitta. As long as I get dollars 4 it, I don't give a monkey's really.

Addicts language

Tuesday 3/8/99

Well it's been nearly a week since I put anything down on paper concerning how Craig is about Craig lately.

It's like my whole outlook has changed. Feel reasonably content and at ease with myself. That's down to a few things, mainly a conversation I had y/d plus a phonecall 2 a girlfriend I have in recovery who I have had no contact with in many months. Today life don't seem so bad. Do feel I'd fare much better if I had solid support from outside like promised, but I'm powerless over these people. My expectations of others is way 2 high, but I'm getting my head round that one, doing a pretty good job of it too. Bit of acceptance that's all it takes... All this bollocks is my cross to bear, no-one else's. Test of my character – simple as that. I look back over what I've written b4 and I smile – I can get so buried in my own head at times – it's the nature of this illness. Total egocentricity... been that way 4 years. Gotta learn 2 laugh at myself more, and not think so deeply about shit.

I'm alive, I'm well, health, got food and a bed, don't need gear to get out of bed, so what have I got to grumble about... even though I'm incarcerated, I'm safe and I'm well and I don't need to use today. Things could be better but they are as they are. Today I look in the mirror and I like what I see – I'm thankful 4 the friends I have in my life 2day. I'm thankful 2 be alive.

I can count the real friends I got on one hand but I don't need many. One in particular makes 10 of any other. God give her me to keep an eye on and vice versa... I honestly think I would not be walking the earth 2day if I didn't have this person in my corner. I'd have met my maker long ago – so 4 that alone I'm grateful she touched my life. Today is a day of gratitude 4 me.

Wednesday 4th/8th/99; 8.30is in the morning

How do I feel? Pretty good really, in fine form considering. Pretty mad 'cos I wrote about gratitutde y/d and at the meeting it was all about gratitude...

Still feel grateful too, normally wears off after 5 minutes. But I'm clinging on to it with dear life. You know, I still feel like I'm actually recovering from the madness in my nut. Feeling peaceful still and I don't wanna lose that yet...I'm doing my step 3 every morning and giving thanks at night, and I feel ok about it. If that's what it takes to keep my nut above water, then I'm up 4 it – not a great sacrifice is it?

It's all up and down. Good p/c with a girl friend the other night – lifted my spirits no end. She's a beautiful woman (could never replace P...), in recovery too, so she know the COO and understands about it all. She wants to come see me too (more than I can say about my multifaceted Gemini pal) so that'll do me good. Keep me in touch with humanity.

Wonder if the fucking postman's saying anything where I'm concerned. Been waiting 4 a couple of tapes off my sister 4 two mth now...had words about it last week, assured me they were coming – still niche!

S'been a sore lesson... feel pretty alone 'cos no-one's really done shit 4 me. I really feel let down but I've let people down all my life – but (again!) two wrongs don't make a right do they? All that cock and bull about being too busy or skint, just don't fit right with me...I'm definitely alright with it though. Took me a while but...it's a case of a learning process 4 me, my expectations of others is way too high, and when not fulfilled I get angry and resentful and it ain't good 4 me.

Everyone's individual and I got no power over anyone (as much as I'd like to have) so I gotta swallow and let it go.

Fefinitely changes things 4 me though, I must say that

It's about me being there 4 me, 'cos no-one else is, regardless of what's said... only I'm responsible so it's my lookout. Can't deny I feel deserted, but just 'cos I feel that way, it don't mean that's how it is, it don't mean it's reality – it's just how I feel – I'm aware of that! But it's affecting how I react to the people I feel have just left me to get on with it.

I really did think J.....would give me more support. Don't know why I feel let down. She's the same as me – wild and unfuckingtameable.

I suppose even guardian angels need time off now and again.

Enough said...

Addicts language

I feel good, I look good, I got another chance – All thanks to my creator.

You know, I don't feel weird or uncomfortable at all saying that, and that spells growth

Yeah man, I grow and mature every day.

Here's a list of 10 things I would like after a year in recovery!

10 things
1. To be happy in myself, self love and self respect
2. A degree of integrity
3. Real friends
4. To be there 4 P..... 4 once
5. Healthy relationships with my family
6. Healthy relationships with J.......... (regardless of what happens)
7. A steady girlfriend
8. A flat
9. A job
10. A car plus driving license

Not a lot to ask 4... (I don't think!!)

Thursday 5th August

Starting to slip – hanging out 4 a letter. Feel disconnected and strange. Tried ringing J..... to no avail. Bollocks to it. Not sure why I'm so hooked into her;

Spent the morning so far in the sun. Feel homesick, can't wait 4 a bit of female company. My balls are tight.

It's like everyday I do a letter wait and nigh on every day I draw a blank.

Friday:

Funny ol' letter off P....y/d. Strange it was. The spell that girl's got over me is crazy. My tactics got a response though, surprised me really! Prison just makes me crazy and twists up my rational mind (as if I got one).

Diary: A Life of Dubious Virtue

Feel proper still – keep wondering when the storm clouds will return.
Nearly picked up a bit of gear y/d. Feel chuffed I never... life's alright considering I'm in the bowels of the system.
Here's a beautiful poem from the Song of Solomon
"My beloved spake and said unto me
Rise up, my love, my fair one and come away....
For lo, the winter is passed, the rain is over..."

Tuesday 10th August

Funny day, not quite sure how I feel! Been restless 4 a day or two – mental dreams and broken sleep. Been years since I slept solid... (without drugs that is).
Woke at 6.30 this morning and I was consumed by jealously. It was right on me...right poxy evil feeling. I got such a dark side to me...it's 4ever there, just waiting to pounce.
The dream was about u know who. Can't remember it, but it was nasty. Sign maybe?
Overall, I'm sweet still.
Doing what I need to be doing
But am I?

Wednesday 18th August 11pm – ish

Gratitude, Gratitude, Gratitude, Gratitude
At this moment in time, I'm in touch with some gratitude.
Thanks to the one who matters for putting people in my life who matter – people who touch me deep inside and don't even know they do it.
I'm just glad 2 be alive and clean, and still with my mind.
And I can feel – and it's alright.
First and 4most, there's P.... That girl lights up my soul. Her spirit burns so bright and she don't even know it.
And there's others still.
I was meant to recover....
How could I not be when I been sent all these beautiful people 2 inspire me.
I can see it all now, just briefly maybe, but I got faith these flashes will eventually merge and I will finally be the <u>man</u> I dreamed of being.....

Today it's ok and I'm full of gratitude and love 4 the people who matter to me and even if they don't know it, I do! And I'll send it out with my thoughts and hopefully in some subtle way – they'll feel it
Who knows?
This programme works...

24/8/99

Been a while since I logged in, so I thought I better do the honours – got a fair bit going on upstairs as it goes.

Well, it's Tuesday morning, and it's pretty fucking dismal (GREY)

It's mad but the weather can affect how I feel – if I let it. So I do feel grey 2day, not blue 'cos I ain't sad or melancholy in any way.

How could I explain the word 'grey' into a feeling – grim? Resigned? Tinge of resentment and bitterness thrown in...

Do I feel all these things 2day?

Not sure really

Do feel resigned about certain issues, yeah? Feel a bit grim, but not sure about the latter 2.

All in all I feel slightly off-centre and that will affect my reactions 2 people if I'm not careful.

It's all about how Craig feels about himself that counts 2day. All the outside stimuli are just superficial stuff 2 avoid looking at the real problem. Coming on leaps and bounds in this respect though. I'm pleased with myself, I'm growing day by day, doors are opening 4 me again, relationships in certain areas are blossoming, yet one in particular seems 2 be waning. I got this feeling it's run its course and that's a shame, 'cos the person is important 2 me. Touches me deeper than she'll ever know.

Been here b4 though and it's revived and got stronger so who knows.

I got no control over what happens. Que sera, sera

Still waiting on blood test results. It's a heavy weight 2 carry, and I can't share it. It's the biggest thing I faced up 2 now. Many late nights and feelings of guilt and shame.

Serious shit really.

Diary: A Life of Dubious Virtue

Think these c***s are taking the piss really. Been waiting 25 days 4 an answer. This don't seem right... it needs rectifying 4 other inmates who suffer the same worry in the near and foreseeable future I don't see it as acceptable and human healthcare...being treated like a second rate citizen. I expressed at the initial counselling session 7 days b4 the actual test (32 days ago?) how much it was weighing me down and so on. Yet since the test, there's been nothing. I've just been left 2 sit with it. No advice or offers 2 talk, nothing. When I've took it on myself 2 chase up, I've met indifference, people 2 busy 2 stop. I was even told not 2 be silly and don't worry. This I don't find acceptable. Maybe the fella didn't realise the implications of what I was asking, but still this is a serious business and the whole system needs looking into.

Been down 2 the nurse and got my results after 35 days of waiting –

HIV negative
Hep B   negative (getting full course of vaccinations)
Hep C   POS   (getting worse)

It's a relief. I can't deny it. Been affecting my behaviour and relationships.

S'all sweet now. Got no excuses. I was more concerned 4 J......... There'd of been no way 2 tell her... but I don't need 2 now.

From now on it's time 2 get responsible. It's a dangerous society in that respect....

KEY WORD   'RESPONSIBILITY'

Wednesday 25th: Feel centred

It's a grey day again, I've not really took it on board though... I feel shredded as it goes.

You can't think yourself into good living. You must live yourself into good thinking and that's what's happening.

I got a bit of self respect back. I feel good and look god.

I respect myself and my living space, and I feel respect 4 others and their space. Don't get returned as much as I'd like, but that's what jail's all about. Poor ignorant fools the majority. Just can't see...

It was like that 4 me 4 a very long time, so I know the depth of the denial.... I'm thankful I've been given the insight 2 change stuff 2day.

And glad I got the courage 2 attempt it – More 2 say but I got an important letter 2 write. And my mind is like a sieve at the moment, been meaning 2 write it 4 days and keep 4getting.

Bank Holiday – 30th August

Another month bites the dust...5 months, 10 days...

Feel a touch off key, know what it's about. Went back 2 bed and woke up 4 kitchange all fucked up, rushed down all over the place – I need 2 get a feel of my self in the morning (that ain't how it sounds). I need 2 know where I'm at b4 I get into shit with the rest of the human race.

It seems 2 me I treat others badly when I feel badly about myself. I believe this....

When I feel good, I give off good stuff. When I'm not clever, if I'm not careful I get into shit with people, I'm intolerant, violent, impatient, angry and so on and so forth. So it's important 4 me 2 be aware of myself.

If I can change my actions, then surely my thoughts will follow? You know, living your way into good thinking.

So it's important 4 me 2 get centred in the mornings, so I know where I'm at and don't get caught unawares by one of these bastards and do something I'm gonna regret....

Last night b4 I dropped off, I was day dreaming I was out 4 a drink in N London with P..., and Gary K and Ellie turned up. We went back 2 Ellie's 4 a drink and that. Gary pulled some gear out. And I was laying there running through all the different scenarios in my mind. I just let it run and run, got right immersed in it.

I was gonna go in the bedroom and leave them 2 it. But I didn't want 2 leave J...... in with 'em 'cos I knew she'd do some. So I said I was leaving. She wouldn't come so I stuck a knife through K....'s hand, stabbed into the table and warned him. In every scenario, I stabbed him and whil I was dreaming it, I was getting right off on it. And in every scenario, she stayed and done gear.

I worry about that girl so much where the gear's concerned. 'Cos she's a borderline addict. Displays all the symptoms man, but nothing's yet <u>really</u> brought her 2 her knees.

And there's no-one I know, and I know 1000s of junkies, who has just played with the gear. Its got one hell of a sting in its tail, and it stings <u>all</u> who dabble – eventually. That's how it's deceitful. It hides 4 years, letting you think you got away with it, then it pounces and it all comes crashing down.

I never worried about someone like I worry about her...She's gonna go her way and that's that. I don't honestly think she's that stupid anyway. Powerless over her. But still I feel a degree of responsibility 4 her... She's my friend. Best friend I ever had.

I take a solemn oath that if I find out Gary K or that fat c*** Ellie keeps turning her on to the tackle, then I'm gonna stab him up. I swear this 2 myself. I'm not violent, but I'm capable of violence. I'd give my life for that girl.

Tuesday 31st August

Funny day

A friend just gone home and I feel quite sad about it 2 tell ya the truth... I don't make many friends. Make many acquaintances, but not friends. You don't meet many warm friendly genuine people in these gaffs, so when I do, I take 2 them. 'Cos that's what I'm about when I'm clean.

So W.....'s off home 2day, I wish him luck, chances are I'll hear no more off him. Once you get out you leave all this behind you and crack on. I probably wouldn't get on the same with him out there. Something about doing time that pulls people 2gether. You lose a common bond when you're released.

It pisses me off 'cos I lose 2 many good friends. I wish him all the best and with luck we won't meet again in another junkie establishment.

So after a good start 2 the day, I feel blue.

Wednesday 1/9/99 (4 moon 2 the year 2000)

Well, nutty day emotionally. I waste my power thinking and obsessing with shit that don't matter rather than living in the moment and seeing it's all ok with Craig in the moment and stay empowered.

Nutter?

J.....e's back from France. That girl's cushty. I get a postcard off her and it was sweet of her 2 be thinking of me all the way over there on holiday. Surprised me. More than J.....'s done in 3 wk. If I didn't put in the effort, we wouldn't communicate at all.

I let her affect me 2 much. I'm bigger than that. Don't know why I waste so much energy thinking about her... that could go elsewhere where needed.

I'm just emotionally unstable and insecure. That's all it's all about.

It's mad 'cos the other day I was writing about a good friend being released on this electronic tagging – HOME CURFEW BALLS: Well, later that night, the poor c*** turned up back on the wing. I had 2 fucking laugh. Poor fella was sitting on the drain drinking a can of nectar and 2 gathers turned up and said he had 2 escort them back 2 prison. Turns out it was a mistake him being released- he wasn't meant 2 be out 4 another 3 days. So the poor fuckers sweating it out across the way again – I know it's cruel but you gotta smile... It's weird 'cos you can be doing a 3 and it'll fly all the way then the last week will be as long as all you've done.

Time just ain't relative when you're in 4 your M O T

Another day done.

Later

Sunday 5/9/99

Feel off key, sad and lonely. Got this yearning 2 be in certain company. Today, I feel there's no hope... at times like this I get in touch with a part of me that's forever been there and forever will be. This deep loneliness is an intricate part of my make up and it can never be fixed, of that I'm certain.

I got this hole inside

I can never connect with other people like normal

There's a part of me that wants to suffer this crushing feeling of being totally isolated and untouched spiritually from other people. I need to suffer

Diary: A Life of Dubious Virtue

I'm definitely sicker than people realise. Everyone has their opinion on what I should or shouldn't do, but no-one feels what I feel... or sees what I see. It's so easy to sit on the sidelines directing...

Monday 6th September

That was y/d and this is 2day – totally different outlook. The mind is a really mental thing – well it is in my case... can only speak 4 myself.

I'll always feel that chasm, that abyss in my soul, but I learn to live with it better as each day goes by. It's just that some days I open myself up to it and a gaze into its depths, and the darkness takes me unawares. I really struggle to pull away again... Y/d was one of them days. It amazes me how shallow I am in regard to needing some things: woman, drugs or clothes and money, to make me feel better. Yet at the same time, I'm so deep, my bottom can't be found. Contradiction in terms??? Test-case drug-addict!!!

I've been aware of the fact I need to buckle down again in regards to my writing. My last ally in recovery is off this week and then I'm back to my lone wolf McQuade act. Not getting the help I though I would from outside – got their shit to contend with... And it's imperative I stay clean while I do this. It's a self esteem issue. And today I'll do whatever it takes, including the simple task of committing myself to an hour's writing about what my life's like in this self-imposed prison cell I've constructed in my nut. Built with bars of guilt, shame, anger, resentment, false pride, jealousy and lust. You know, I'm fully aware that till I can smash these bars down, I'll never be free of myself. Had a fair bit of realisation today. I'm doing another written step one and one of the questions was as follows:

Q:

I've done things while acting out on my addiction that I would never do when focusing on recovery. What were they?

Well, an example came up I hadn't thought about b4. The time I was with J... all day, everything was cushty, yet I bumped into someone who was going to score, so fuck the consequences, I was off. Argued with P..... had no regard 4 her feelings at all. I came back after doing gear, got drunk, took speed. P... was outside the club but I went home with this old slapper and fucked her. I think I told J.... the next day or something. Done her head I suppose. Never really, really though about it till today, not from her side, trying to feel what she felt. Must of hurt her. No wonder she don't trust me.

The prime examples of powerlessness over drugs – everything was sweet, was having a better day with someone I care 4 deeply, but yet I chose to act out and ruin it 4 gear.

Then a prime example of unmanageability: out of my nut and sleeping with someone I don't really want to sleep with when someone I really want is nearby.

Proper c*** really and I must of wrecked her head at the time. These are things I must look at. She's a soldier yeah, but still she must have had feelings around it. It's only now I can see that.

I tell myself I slept with the slut 'cos J... told me at the station (in her drama queen role) ;that that was it. So I could easily justify my actions. But its bollocks. I slept with the girl 'cos my head was done in... fixed my feelings... When all I had to do was talk to P....

Too late now, and I'm not saying different, but for my own sake and the sake of future relationships, I need to see my triggers and short circuit the prideful acting out.

I'm not a dirty dog really, even though my past record spells otherwise. I got the potential to be a slut, but I no longer have to act out on it if I don't wanna, whereas b4 I would get hard and there'd be no stopping me.

Don't mean nothing to me no more (U Fucking Liar !!! – Yeah man, maybe it does but I know that's just a jail thing as your senses are bombarded by pretty girls on the tele and in mags, and you become acutely aware you're starved of them. But I just don't get turned on by any bird no more, must be getting choosy in my old age.

Everything's cushty anyway

Relaxed as can be.

J......e's back from France by now, so I should get a letter 2morrow maybe. The girl's a good one. I'm a lucky c*** in that sense. Why are all my friends female. Do you think I've got a hidden agenda? Must admit it is convenient. Only buzzing

I better sign off 4 now. I got 2 get ready 4 badminton.

Tuesday 7th September

Well, it's 8.30 in the morning, been up and showered 4 an hour now. Looks like we got a day behind the door 2day. Just been round and locked us up 4 some reason. Don't bother me – if I'm being put in jail then the best way 2 do it is 23 hr bang up. That way you just block out what's really happening in the world and live out your time in this bubble.

I'd prefer it if your food got put through a hatch in the door too – less contact as possible.

Here's a couple of poems/songs I really like.

I'm only you by Robyn Hitchcock

~Said I'm a willow, bending in your mind
I'm a mirror cracked from side 2 side
I'm a snow covered mountain in an empty room
I'm a house that burns down every night
4 you
Said I'm a doorway leading 2 the dark
I'm a liquid yawn dissolving
I'm a policeman working in an empty house
I'm a distant steeple on a long abandoned plane
Sometimes, when I'm lonely, baby, then I'm only you.
Said I'm a pattern on a china bowl
I'm a memory engraved upon your soul
I'm a prison cell without a door
I'm a finger drawing on a frosty window pane
Sometimes when I'm lonely baby, then I'm only you.

I'll write the other one another time. Pucka lyrics.

Thursday 9th September

Life's pretty good. Regardless of the fact I'm in the garage, it's definitely a rollercoaster ride though... But the lows ain't as frequent. It's like everything is sorta levelling out. 60 days without anything. I'm impressed with myself. My self esteem grows daily. I'm looking good and feeling good. Today my middle name is 'Mustard'.

OK, what can I say today.

I'll keep my expectations of friends and family at a reasonable level. I gotta remember others are only human and prone to mistakes same as I am.

All my life I was a human 'doing' not 'being', but 2day I'm just a human 'being' and it's good. I like it.

Payday. Bit of snout, noodles, chilli, P.L's. Got this urge to ring someone but I'll hold off. Why waste credits when people can't even write? Save my money.

WELL FUCKING WELL???

Friday's upon us once again! Long w/e, they hurt. Weekdays fly but them w/es.. boy, do they hurt.

Been a while since I logged in, been a mental ride. My nut has been all over the place. Still weighed in but I've just given up sweating about shit. So as you can guess, I'm back into a 'take it easy' mode.

As long as I stay off the tabackle I'm doing the business.

I just got back from gym, shit session. So I had myself a little cell 'makeover'. Now I'm gonna bounce in the shower. Then I'll write 4 a bit. Just see where the pen takes me, see how I'm feeling.

I was just sitting here, goofing off, running through things in my head – as you do!! (seems like a long time since I have). When I don't think about shit objectively, I become nuts. I need 2 write and speak about the reality of things 2 remain sane.

Anyway, as I was saying, I was just running through stuff and I realised how resilient and optimistic I am. S'not often I look at my assets and acknowledge the ability I have 2 smile in the face of adversity..

September 28th

Good day y/d. Definitely beginning 2 see the growth in myself. Still a long way 2 go but it's alright. Pain is growth.

Excellent letter y/d. Only the 2nd in 5 weeks. Worth waiting 4 though.

I awake every morning hopeful... I know it was a good letter 'cos I enjoyed writing back.

Everyday I wait 2 hear if I'm moving 2 another jail. I need another move.

Is it a progressive move?

Have 2 wait and see...

Anyway, I'm eating well, feeling well, looking well, all's well...

September 30th

1st waking thought this morning was a feeling of relief and then some gratitude kicked in. I wouldn't say my thinking is straight and true but I know enough 2 know I don't want 2 wake up sick 4 heroin again. I felt so happy and optimistic this morning – still do. I haven't really thought of the many hundreds of times I've awoke filled with dread 'cos I got nothing 2 cook up and stick in my vein.

If I can hold on 2 how I feel 2day and the memories of days gone by while stuck in a habit, I stand a chance.

I am grateful it ain't like that 2day. Even though it may be just a brief respite. Any respite will do 4 me.

It's my choice how long the respite lasts...

8/10/99

Roll on the 22

Feel strong and as positive as I possibly can be about my future. 2 ways I can look at it. I can see it as a bleak prospect, A lonely cold struggle 2 reach death. Or a bright new chapter full of wonder and new frontiers just waiting 2 be discovered. Today I'm an intrepid traveller... I can't wait.

For the 1st time in my life I feel let down and disappointed in J..... I see her 4 what she is – a human. Maybe that's a good thing as painful as it is.

I have 2 be aware of the fact that thinking you're right about something can leave you bitter. It's hard though, 'cos I'm driven by pride.

I really need 2 reach out 4 the company and attention of a bird. I love women. They are the most amazing creatures on earth. I got birds I can ring or write, but the only one (apart from Pilch) I want 2 connect with is P.... But that's not happening.

Addicts language

She's on a different trip – light yrs from me. I got acceptance around it now.

Leaves me blue though, but I won't feed her ego no more....

4 the 1st time in my life, I see that the friendship we got is nowhere near as strong and stable as I though it was. And I can see it's been in decline 4 a while now.. but you lose one special friend and gain another. That's occurring... but P could never be replaced.

Wednesday 13th October

Just under 4 moon left now. Seems 2 be speeding up a bit... Roll on Xmas. I gotta bit to write today; been neglecting it a bit.

It's like everyday I wait 4 news off of a certain person and even though I know that person just ain't interested in writing me really... I still wait and hope. Is that nuts or what? Got nothing better 2 do though. She might come round?! How does that make me feel? Dunno! Not good...

I'll return to this in a minute....

No news.

It's now about 6p.m. I got a meeting to go to tonight. Got nothing better to do. Finding this really ahrd work. Doing my best to keep a level head and hold it down, but my handle on it all is slipping. All the old insanity is taking a hold again. Not sure what's real and what's not. (My support network just ain't there, 4 whatever reasons people are comfortable with). I never experienced such a feeling of powerlessness b4. I like 2 have a say in what direction my life and relationships go in. It's a funny situation 2 be in really. You know I have to be right careful on how I react to situations and examples of powerlessness because my view on life and people is very often distorted. So I'm just really having to contain myself. So I got all this stuff going on that I just can't talk about. Therefore, I'm a walking timebomb. I begin to tell myself I need gear to diffuse my self from exploding. I'm falling out with people all the time.

Gear ain't gonna solve shit. This is something I just gotta get through and ride it all the way. I refuse to pick up 2day. I'm told that all pain is emotion, all growth. Not sure if I believe that one. But maybe I needed to feel this one to get a true sense of perspective on the depth of the relationships in my life. By relationships, I mean the people who really matter in my life.

I'm gonna break off 4 10 minutes 'cos I got a bit of washing to do... (turning into a right domesticated twat). I enjoy bussing about and keeping things all straight and clean. S'about slef-respect.

Don't get me wrong; if I got someone to do it 4 me then I'll just sit back and let 'em crack on, but I'm more than capable of looking after myself...

I used to be able to write very eloquently. It was a talent I had. I could express with a pen more than I could with my tongue. It's like the pen was a part of me... and the thoughts would just flow fluently, gently overlapping, one leading to the other and so on..without me consciously being aware of it. Like the pen had it's own consciousness and I just helped it do it's thing... And I think it was 'cos, even though I was 'bad' (or whatever society labels me as being), I had this innocence or naivety around my thinking. I had this ability to see into the grey areas of life as opposed to just black and white.

I've gone through life on autopilot, not really experiencing any of the experiences I've had. And I've done more than most and met many interesting people along the way – good and bad. But the extensive drug use that I was involved in denied me the opportunity of _really_ experiencing these people and places on an emotional level.

'Cos I never really felt the joy or pain of these encounters, they had no real impact or effect on the person I was to become... Do you see where I'm coming from?

I got so much more to say, yet I got shit to do. I'll return to this.

November 4th

Seems like an 'eon' since I last logged in: probably 'cos it is, aye?.

Things are sweet at the moment, was an uphill struggle 4 a while there, but we seem 2 have reached the crest of the hill and it's all levelled out, 4 now anyway.

Things are pretty rosy in all areas. 12 weeks or so to go. Don't know what I'm doing yet really – know what I'd like to do but it don't just involve me so we'll have to see how things are come Feb. S'not I'm stuck 4 things to do. I got a healthy fear mixed with quite a bit of excitement.

This is the best it's been 4 me mentally and emotionally...

Like I say, been an uphill struggle but starting to see the value of staying off – fucking boring.

'J...'s opened it all up but I ain't holding my breath...

Been having some really good sessions of late with my 'spiritual' guide – seriously, she's good stuff, helps me get right in touch with stuff. And I need that.

It takes courage to really look at yourself.

My b/d soon – 30 yrs of age... still feel 18 really. Got my bounce back... Be right nice to see P...., but it ain't worth even going there with my thinking.

The world's my oyster...so I can't fool my self into thinking I want this and that. Just 'cos I ain't got it!!! Bottom line is I don't know what I want... this is all new ground to me. I'm not bothered if certain things go pear-shaped, as it's a new chapter and I feel it's my time to flourish...Put all the last 10 yr behind me once and 4 all. Been a lost decade 4 me in all areas of my life.

November 5th

I feel quite blue and a bit emotional? Is it strange 4 a man to make such a statement? I don't think it is – 2 years ago I'd of attached stigma to these feelings – but not today.

I've seen another good pal go today (Paul) and that's a joyous occasion really, as the poor sod's done 4 out a 6. So this is one hell of a day 4 that man – close the chapter finally on a tragic mistake...I feel sad. Not to see him go but 4 the loss of a friend. Given more time, I could of easily put him into that category.

Of all the hundreds of shady mixed-up people you meet while you float through the system, all but a few will instantly be 4gotten the moment your eyes break contact with theirs...but there's a few that connect on an intimate level – where you share stuff – real stuff- about the pain of this existence.

I seem 2 have said goodbye 2 many times – so it just gets me in touch with that part of myself that's eternally hurting.

4 a ruthless c***, I'm quite an emotional person

Just a mass of contradictions...
I wish the man well....

"May the grass grow green beneath his feet,
May the wind be behind him
And may the sun shine 4ever on his back
Peace, love, and life Paul
Hope u get what you want

Another door closed....

Now all I want is to get to Ashwell and focus on getting the Xmas hurdle done and dusted ... Then it's the home straight... The I close this book (once and 4 all we hope!). And I can finally wipe my mouth of it all and look to the sky.

Life is so, so mad! But I fucking love it – Pain and all.

J...'s been on my nut. I know how 2 drop it from now on. I found this room in my head that I once occupied but 4 some uncertain reason I decided 2 vacate (many years ago) even though I was comfortable there. Anyway, I've had the luck of rediscovering I'm that person still.

I really want 2 look out the window and watch the man walk out of all this in one piece with his head high... But its his moment not mine. I'll write some more soon.

6/11/99

S'gonna be a mad day... emotionally anyway – 'cos that's the only madness I experience lately. Phone call y/d to her has sparked this off... I'm so off it at times. Things r smooth but I know they ain't really – not deep down.

Friday 19th November

Been 2 weeks or so since I wrote. A right nutty 2 weeks 2... Up and down. I must be sick 'cos I just attract all the sickos and I know they are sickos 'cos they gotta be sick 2 give me the time of day. I mean, people in the real world...

Not got a lot 2 really say...

Just logging in, marks off more time in my nut. Dow 2 3 months, less even. Matter of weeks. Don't matter where I go or what I do... it's gonna be OK. I have got someone I'd like 2 go and spend time with, but we'll see how it progresses. It's cool at the moment, but time changes everything. So we'll wait with baited breath and see.

It'll be OK no matter what I do as long as I don't listen 2 that voice that wants 2 destroy me. " We all do what we can, and it has 2 be good enough... and if it isn't good enough, it hs 2 do. Nothing is ever lost, that cannot be found."

26th November 1999

OK, been a week since I logged in; not much has happened really but at the same time much has happened.

I got a bit 2 comment on, my thoughts on my future, the way the relationships in my life are going, my mental state and well being and son and so forth.

I been thinking about my future a lot. I need 2 be.

I get a lot of good feedback off a close friend. Seems all I normally get is criticism and my problem is I take on too much of what others think. And they should spend their mental energy looking at themselves and sorting out their own lives...

At this moment in time, I got so much self belief and a strong sense of my capabilities. I <u>know</u> what I'm capable of.. I hold myself well and I attract what I need. I know it'll come 2 me, all I want is there 4 the taking if I stay off the powders and just keep cool and be patient. No more forcing the issue... I ain't your average joe, I gotta little something extra. I still got a fair bit 2 learn but I'm like a sponge, I'm so receptive, man.

This ain't arrogance speaking, it's my heart. I'm a humble, open-minded, honest fella at heart. All this uphill slog and battle I've been fighting is at an end. In 10 weeks, it's time 4 the end result. It's mke or break time... I've a fear that I'll end up alone and broke and there's nothing 4 me out there. But I'm not gonna let fear rule my life no more.

I got this sense of I'm made 4 good things and I think it's time 2 collect.

So how are the relationships in my life?

The family; well, there's growth... I'm doing the right thing so it can only get better. Simple as that. As long as I do right by them, there's no problem is there? I'm awaiting a letter off my sister at the moment. I want her thoughts on it all. I trust her judgement above every ones... I need 2 know where she sees me going from here? Does she think I'm up 4 this?

I understand there is cynicism on all behalfs. It will take a lot 2 prove myself 2 my family. And really, M..... is the sum total of my family. And the only one I got anything 2 prove 2, apart from myself. The rest can go take a flying fuck. I'm either accepted or fuck 'em. No conditions will do.

I've sorta realised my dad is not a man I can rely on... Never has been b4 so why should it change?

P...'s OK, things have changed. She's good stuff, but my awareness of myself and others is such that I know by how it is that a great chance is coming. And our friendship is coming 2 a close. It's a struggle all the time lately. I'm aware enough 2 feel it and sense it.

I'm hypersensitive you see! It's the end of an era 4 us... The distance becomes greater every day. I used 2 have a spiritual connection with the girl, but it's fading. I see her differently. She'll always have a place in my heart.

Bit melodramatic but I see a bit deeper than most...I'm not sure if it's a gift or a burden, but it's how it is. She can't see we are clutching at straws, but I can. Be nice 2 see her sort herself out though.

So, how am I feeling?

Self assured, confident of my abilities, excited, refreshed, frustrated and fearful of failure. It's gonna be OK

J.....e is an interesting girl. I never knew how interesting really, only just dawning on me... She makes me feel alive...She's only a friend but I know it's got prospects.

How much do I value her friendship? Enough not 2 fuck her? I don't know. She's a vulnerable girl and has an c**** when it comes 2 all that. So I got 2 think it through seriously...

I care bout her. It's mad but I know I do 'cos of how I think 2wards her. She makes my conscience speak 2 me. Definitely chemistry, but I don't know what I want so would it be fair? I think I'd just slaughter her. It's in my nature.

Mine and P....'s friendship was strong enough 4 us 2 fuck about like that. Something we needed 2 do. And I'm glad we did.

Addicts language

I just understand the true value of friendship 2day. It's everything. Without friends I have my life would be meaningless.

All in all life's cool. I'm cool, feeling groovy, and reflective. Proud!!!

Been a struggle 2 get where I am in my head 2day. I'm not going back 2 where I came from. Not 2day.

Having grief with the Powers that Be but I just gotta remember not 2 take it personal.

December 4ᵗʰ 1999: Saturday 9am

Well, it's a fucking glorious morning outside and I – sunshine in my soul and I won't question it – just soak up the rays while it lasts. I've come 2 realise I'm a morning man through and through.

By 1ish, that initial euphoria about being alive is fading fast. Only fades, 'cos the negativity of the environment weighs heavy on your shoulders – it's a struggle 2 keep it at bay no matter who you think you are... I do OK though most days.

I'm doing my time respectably, if such a thing can be possible.

The sky has all of a sudden gone grey and overcast! A sign? An example of how things can switch in the blink of an eye, everything is looking fine and dandy, turn your back 4 a second and bam!!! That's how life is...

I've been sitting looking out at the blue sky, watching the birds flitting 2 and fro. It amazes me how I can derive so much pleasure from such simple things. A true reflection on hwo I am deep down...

So, what can I tell you 2 update my present situation?

There's stuff 2 say, don't know where I'll start though. Not that it's 2 complicated really. Complicated enough though. I wonder shy I need my relationship situation 2 be complicated. Not sure if it is? Which is a lie as I wrote it, I thought 'Liar.'

Still no news off M..... Surprises me really 2, but she's a busy girl. I got a feeling I'll hear off her 2day actually, if not 2day, then this week.

Out of everyone, her opinion on things matters most. Not that I don't value P...'s opinion – I just trust my sister's judgement implicitly. She walks the walk daily and I can't fault her 4 that. Not that she can tell me anything I don't already know deep down...

Time is ticking away now – under 10 weeks 2 go. 67 day exactly. Time 4 me to go about getting it all right in my head. This chapter is finally coming 2 a close. I've put my application 4 help off NACRO in the system now. Waiting game now. Nothing else we can do really is there? I'll be OK

I'm gonna sign off and watch the football 4 a bit. I still got a fair bit to say really.

It's now Monday morning – I was up at half 7, feel fucking pukka really. Sor of smiley inside – it's really a relief 2 be waking fee of the obsessions 4 chemicals. 2day my obsession 4 pussy; just hope I don't get 2 unmanageable arount it.

Back in 2 seconds; gotta just get a V.O. out in the post...

I'm aching all over at the moment, my back, shoulders, arms, top of legs – feels sweet though.

Time 2 kick the gym up a bit, tighten right up. My bum needs 2 be tighter.

Well, another w/e bites the dust, 3 left till Xmas, 8 left till I'm out – 8 – can't adam and eve it really.

P... let me down around the phone again. She don't mean nothing by it, just don't think. I do care about the girl but my nut's wandering elsewhere. The girl can't even get it 2gether to take a phone call. Sure, I'm gonna get another blinding excuse again this week... If she's anything like me, she'll come up with one. I got no choice 2 believe – not that it matters really. S'up 2 her at the end of the day. I got nothing on her – that much is obvious. I jest got a gut feeling she's far 2 unmanageable emotionally 4 me 2 even consider being around...

Me and Janine have kicked it up a gear, and I don't know what 2 do about it really. I do really like her. 1st bird that's ever stimulated my mind the way P... once did... She's everything a man could want; cute, sexy, gorgeous, blonde, funny, sensible....

But is it what I really want. I know it's there 4 me, and I care about her a lot. It's got a lot of promise I think. Maybe she's the one – I don't know!

I just don't want 2 hurt her. I can hear my conscience whispering...Watch this space, I suppose...

What else can I tell ya?

Not a lot really... So I'll leave it there 4 this week.

8 w/e's 2 go.

Friday 16th December

60 days 2 go

Feeling; fine, focused and centred...

Bit sad over the situation with J...... such is life. It hurts 2 lose a friend but I think its gonna happen... I hope not and only time will tell... we'll see.

She'll always be a friend – only true one I've ever had, but the intimacy has gotta stop. It's not fair on her... or Janine. I want to be true to who I'm with.

Just waiting 2 go 2 a circuit. My fitness is coming along a treat. Proud of myself...

Finally got through 2 Janine y/d. Was driving me ad. All seems well. I'll wee her Sunday. Can't come soon enough. Everything is cool really, apart from P... I don't know? It's her call. Today I'm gonna ring Mandy.

17 days till year 2000

Tuesday 14th 12th 1999

So what can I say 2 day then? About a week since I last logged on, bottomed right out since then... and now I'm on the way up again... Women are the bane of my life, but I can't live without them. I'm hoping I get some news off my No 1 but I got a feeling... We'll see... There's times I should look back and read this, but I just don't want 2. It serves its purpose as it is... Maybe in a few years if I make it that far...

My gym is coming along nicely, can see the benefits as well as feel them... So that's driving more. Less than 60 days and I'm out. 57 2 be exact. My time 4 a rerun is coming. I don't know what 2 do about J..., but it'll make itself clear when it's time 2 know. I honestly don't give a fuck if she's bad 4 me or not. I'd risk the lot 4 a while with her. Until she makes it plain 2 me I ain't wanted about, then she's fucking stuck with me....

I gotta be patient with her, that's all and I will be. I'll still do what I'm doing, 'cos life goes on but I'll show her I'm there 4 here if she needs me. And maybe, just maybe, one day she'll decide 2 turn it around – who knows.

I got so much 2 sort out really. Need 2 get it all right in my head. A place to stay, a job (eventually), bit of education... The place 2 stay is important...

3 Days to 2000

28/12/99: Bank Holiday Tuesday

Been a while since I logged on. I apologise, I just ain't had the inspiration at all.

I write when I feel I need 2 and 2day I need 2...

So, what can I tell ya?

In a lot of ways everything has been really well – things are looking brighter 4 me every day – I got 44 days (approx) remaining. I feel better in all departments than I ever have. Still got a lot of improvements 2 make but I'm going in the right direction...

Me and Janine are getting on like bread and butter – she's a sexy bird – witty and intelligent 2 boot. Who knows where it'll go? I know she's good 4 me. Best thing 2 come into my life 4 a long time.

I do really like her; 2 what degree I've yet 2 find out but I know she's got a place in my heart.

The phone call with J... has disturbed me. I care 4 that girl so much. To hear her distressed does me, especially when I'm the cause of distress.

What are the odds on me kicking this habit I wonder? Maybe it's best I left her alone. Best 4 her anyway. I don't want 2 fuck her up anymore than she is... She'd stand 4 having me around whatever shape I was in and that ain't fair on her. I gotta be sure I'm completely sincere about all I do in my dealings with her. She's the best friend I've ever or will ever have. I owe it 2 her 2 do right by her.

4:1:2000

A new Millenium! A fresh opportunity to go in a new direction. In 38 days I got a fresh start and I feel good about it.

Addicts language

That's the 90s well and truly buried 4 me.

The good memories 4 me are few and far between – I can count them on one hand, but there's good times ahead.

Now it's getting close, all the pieces are falling into place... it's coming 2gether. Faith is all it took – at times blind faith, but faith all the same!!

J.... seems 2 have come through 4 me... I was worried there 4 a bit but I knew she would deep down. The poor cow is just running scared, and who can blame her? Look at my history?

But she's there still – good as gold as always. I <u>will not</u> fail! 4 her sake if anything. I got the desire 2 stay clean 4 myself but if it goes (the desire that is...) I'll just focus on P....) Can't let my loved one's down no more...

She says I can come stay at hers! What do ya think? I'm buzzing really. Best news so far... My odds improve greatly. Gotta keep it simple but simple is my middle name at the moment.

Four days into a new century and I can already see a new dawn on the horizon of my life...

I'm excited. More so at the prospect of spending time with the best friend I ever had. Getting reacquainted at showing her all her energy has been 4 a good valid reason

<u>I will not fail myself or Pem will not</u>

I'm not even entertaining the thought of failure... Failure is not part of the equation... Why should it be? No reason 4 it 2 be, is there?

31/1/00

Well, that's month no 1 done and dusted. 10 days and I'm outa here...

Took a fair bit 2 talk myself into writing a bit, been nigh on a month since I wrote in here.

Anyway, here I am, on the final le of the journey. I'm just sitting back, taking it easy, stress-free and playing it cool. It's now over. In 11 days I walk away a free man again and I'm buzzing. Feel full of myself. My life has never looked so bright 2 me.

I can't explain how it feels. Feels like I finally came out the other side... feels like I finally found myself a place in life and soon and felt I'm worthy of all I encounter, and more. Much more than I've allowed myself up till now.

I haven't really got a thing 2 worry about and that worries.

Even though it's all set 2 run, I still think there's a pitfall. It's gotta sneak up on me along the line somewhere. Can't have got off that lightly. I just can't get complacent.

Can't get complacent... can't

I feel good about myself at the moment and that's all that counts... and it'll go from strength 2 strength I'm sure.

We started something that can't be stopped

All I want 2 do is have a week off from thinking about it and enjoy myself. And that's what I intend 2 do.

5
NA Meetings

Standing up and being counted

The following work is based on Narcotics Anonymous (NA) meetings that I attended, each one consisting of an army of lost souls. Their stories are all very similar; I dare say some readers will think the whole book is repetitive and that is true, but by the same token we are all individuals and the message in 'Addicts Language', hopefully, will be reinforced by the amount of suffering that I experienced at these meetings. The thing that strikes you the most is the strength that many find at NA meetings and of course the reason behind this is that everyone in the room knows exactly what the person sitting next to them is going through. Most of them call it 'The Illness'; most of them talk of fear and a huge gaping hole inside of them that can only be filled by drugs. They talk of the confidence that only drugs could give them—the feelings of inner peace that they absolutely craved for. They talk about the people that they have hurt, their own arrogance for thinking that they could handle it and control it and then, finally, they talk about the utter devastation it causes and how they wish to God they had never taken drugs in the first place. A young man sitting directly to my right disagreed with them; he said, "I didn't take drugs for any other reason than I wanted to, I wasn't in pain, I wasn't trying to fill a gaping hole inside of me. I was already selling drugs and I was curious to know what it felt like, so many people were prepared to do anything to buy their gear that I just had to find out why."

    The one thing that stands out more than anything is their total honesty. Isn't it strange how people who can lie and deceive the people closest to them, people who would steal from their own mothers can be so totally honest when they have finally hit rock bottom. In every case that I've seen, they only get to this point when there is nowhere further down to go. Only then will they stand up and be counted.

NA Meetings; Bethnal Green

If anyone had told me that I would be going to NA meetings, I would have said "no way"; the nearest I have come to taking drugs was a few puffs of a joint years ago, just to see what it was like (I didn't like it). Since my son and my sister have been ill I have changed so much as a person I can honestly say it is for the better. Writing this book has taught me so much. The people I've met are nothing like I expected them to be. They are no different to you or I, other than they have had a big addiction. At the end of the meeting, we all joined hands; the diversity of the meetings is amazing. All cultures, all walks of life, rich or poor, it matters not; if addiction is gonna get you, it will.

If I were to tell some of the people I know that I have been to NA meetings, they would be horrified, but to write a book and tell it how it really is you must do your groundwork. Meeting these people, each with their own tragic story, I could actually feel their pain and that is what provides the inspiration and the determination to be up at 6.30am, writing day in and day out. If this book even manages to make a few people think twice before experimenting with drugs then it will have been worth the effort. I know that. If you remember when I first met Emma, we gave each other a copy of the Serenity Prayer and when we held hands at the end of each meeting, we all said the Serenity Prayer together. They did this at every meeting we attended.

The Serenity Prayer

God grant us the serenity
To accept the things we cannot change
The courage to change the things we can
And the wisdom to know the difference

Over and over again

Tony chaired the meeting at Bethnal Green. He spoke very honestly about how hard he finds staying clean. The people, about 30 of them, know him. He has helped them all in the past, they all respect him. Em's sister asked to speak at the end of the meeting. She said what brave people they all were. Em went and asked Tony if I could read a poem to them. I told them that my name is Georgie and that I have a son who is starting to get his life back together after 14 years of schizophrenia and if he could come back from his hell then so could they. I wished them all the luck in the world. I read "Caught Within the Headlights" A lot of them came up and talked to me and said that they were pleased that I was writing the book. One of those who told his story said that he had buried three brothers all through drugs. This poem is about just a few that stood up and bared their souls. It's very easy to judge people, but as I sat there I thought about the many times that I have found it so hard to cope with the pain of watching my son's suffering and I couldn't help thinking that if I had access to something like heroin that would transport me from it for just a little while, would I have been strong enough to resist? After meeting so many whose lives have been wrecked, yes I would. But life is a learning process and hindsight is a wonderful thing. In retrospect I can't say in all honesty "no I would not" simply because, like so many, I knew nothing about it. Maybe I would have just seen it as a way to fix my feelings like so many others do.

Over and Over Again

My name is Chris I'm an addict
He stands up and bears his soul
He talks of his sordid addiction
And how getting clean is his goal
My name is Sam I'm an addict
I'm sick of my wasted life
She tells how she once was a mother
And how a good man left his wife
My name is John I'm an addict
This one was the worst of them all
He talked about burying three brothers
So painful for him to recall
For his mother's sake he must make it
To try to make up for her pain
My name is Tanya I'm an addict
Over and over again

Thanks To NA

He stared straight ahead his voice was strong
His wife sat by his side
He'd put it behind him completed 12 steps
His heart was bursting with pride
My neighbour says good morning to me
He thought I was druggie scum
He respects the fact that I'm clean and says
"I knew you could do it son"
My mum says she sleeps like a baby now
For years she'd laid there awake
She's no longer scared of that knock on the door
What a difference NA can make
The guilt's still there, I just hope it will fade
I'm clean at least for today
It's all thanks to God and the love and support
I've found at last at NA

Letter to my addict

While Emma was in rehab, she sent me some work written by some of the others in there. These are their real names and they didn't mind them being used. I had to choose two of the pieces that she sent me. She said that they are all asked to write a letter to their addict.

It was hard to choose which ones to use, one in particular is a whole life story and included poem called 'Beaten and Broken' which I decided to use. The other was written by a young man who wrote it in prison and is called 'Cell Thief'

Beaten and broken

So full of fear, I feel so alone
A baby inside me still hasn't grown
The worlds so unsafe, I just don't belong
So lonely, so beaten, it's all gone so wrong
Where once there was hope, my innocent eyes
Are now full of fright with a head full of lies
My pain is my weakness, I mustn't be seen
A world shrunk in darkness, cold and mean
Help me find shelter, build me a wall
My heart screams, 'please help me'
Can you hear it call?
I can't go on, its all got too much
Some one from somewhere give me a crutch
Come to me now, help to hide me away
Keep me alive, keep me today
Where terror and torment can't twist my head
When deep down inside I'm feeling so dead
I can't reach out because no one will hear
No one to help me no one to get near
I'm slipping away so scared and so broken
Now I'm consumed, no words are spoken
Please end my pain, take it away
The smell and the stench of human decay
The waste, I am blind, can't see any more
Just needles and dealers and going to score

Addicts language

The drugs don't work, my world is black
My only solution, the smack and the crack
My face stained with tears, my life ebbs away
My family before me know not what to say
My hand reaches out no words anymore
My mouth hangs open, please no more
Death please find me, take me away
Please take my life, no more, no way

By   Robert Bushell

Cell thief

I'm down and out in London
The year is 1990
I'm starting on a three-year stretch in Bentonville you see
I was sitting on my cold hard bed
Unable to sleep last night
When my tired eyes beheld a very eerie sight
Something dark and hairy slipped beneath the door
Quietly it made its way across the cold grey floor
I tried real hard to focus on this intruder to my house
Then it became real clear to me the intruder was a mouse
He made his way beneath my bed to where my goodies were stored
Chose for himself a milky way
Then reached for something more
I did not mind the milky way
I had two more you see
But when he took my last half ounce
He made an enemy
I rose up from my freezing bed
As quiet as I could
I stepped right out behind him
He froze right where he stood
I threw a lovely round house
Which connected to his jaw
Grabbed him in a vice like grip
And I hurled him at the door

N A Meeting

I was about to apply the pressure
Which would bring on his demise
Then I saw two tiny teardrops
Appearing around his eyes
He said, 'come on Mr Convict,
Come on take my life
Coz being a mere prison mouse
Has been all hell and strife
I was born and bred in Brixton
My father was a rat
He used to beat me badly
But I shan't go into that
I jumped a sweatbox heading north
Then I wound up stuck in here
They put me in a fraggle cell
And I've lived in constant fear
He had me stealing smokes from cells
When the cons were all asleep
He tattooed Liam on my arm
He was such an evil creep'
The mouse then pulled his fur back
Right back from his paw
There was a skull and hammer
With his number on and all
Now on hearing the mouse's story
I felt real sad to say the least
I wiped the tears from round his eyes
Then let my hands release

written by Liam O'Reilly

NA Meetings: Grays

Relapse

Her head was bowed, her hair was long
She spoke in muffled tones
She talked of the sadness, the years of regrets
And how she hates living alone
She spoke of her shame, her low self-esteem
And an ever-gaping hole
She detested her life, she despised her own self
She revealed her desolate soul
Stripped naked of any dignity
Would her shattered life ever mend
She sat down and sobbed uncontrollably
She'd relapsed last weekend.

One thing I have to say to anyone who is serious about getting clean—go to NA; take the 12 steps of recovery and always remember at every meeting you will meet people who have been clean for years and years and yet they still attend. Why? Because it's a constant reminder of all the people who are just about to take their first step in recovery and a constant reminder of all the pain they are in—pain that they have all experienced and it's witnessing that pain that will help. Paul has, like me, been astonished by the honesty of recovering addicts. It's as if all the lying and deceit that's gone on in the past, along with the years of denial, no longer has a place in their lives. The only way they can get clean and redeem themselves is to bare their souls to each other and to themselves and start a whole new life. We found it very interesting that "God" is so prevalent in the 12 steps, but this is only a good thing. God is good. These people are cleansing their souls and I firmly believe that they will come out of all this hell a far better human being than they went into it. People at NA meetings have stopped blaming the whole world for the devastation they have inflicted, both to their own lives and to the many others around them. They are finally finding their true selves and learning to love their true selves by "standing up and being counted".

Temptation

One at a time is the only way
Each hour, each minute, each second
We strive to stay clean for another day
Many times temptation has beckoned
Fight back, ignore it, and defy it
Don't allow temptation in
You'll be full of regrets in the blink of an eye
If you allow it to win
Temptation wears a sly disguise
Its camouflage is good
If you fail to recognise it
You won't see the trees for the wood
It waits in the wings to barter
Your life for a quick sensation
Look beyond it's evil demeanour
And don't give in to temptation

Words

Words express emotions, they explain the way we feel
A testament to prove that what's happening is real
Words can bring great comfort for the hardships found in life
They tend our wounds to deal with the sharp edge of the knife
Words are always there for us to help with how we're feeling
We can read them and digest them and let them do the healing
They're a friend who's always there for us to help us reach our goal
Words will calm the spirit, words will heal the soul
Words can make us stronger if we read them and digest
Words will help us win when we face our hardest test
Imprint them on your being, feel them in your heart
Words will never let you down so see that from the start
Words will never hurt you or act as judge and jury

Addicts language

They will help you with your sadness and calm your inner fury
Keep them close within your reach, read them loud and make them heard
A trusted loyal and helpful friend, you will always find in words

6
The Case Of Penelope Pittstop

As Bad As Life Can Get

I really thought I'd heard it all by going to NA meetings and witnessing so many bare their souls and talking to so many families whose lives have been so badly affected by drug addiction and with this book almost ready to be sent to the publisher, I'd started to breathe a sigh of relief. Then, right out of the blue came the case you are about to read. The case of Penelope Pittstop, not her real name of course. This is the name she gave to police when they arrested her time and time again, sometimes for shoplifting, soliciting and clipping. For those of you who, like me have no idea what that means—it means taking money for sex and then running off without delivering the goods. When they asked for a name she'd say "Penelope Pittstop"

She was born on August 17th 1970 and her mother says that the doctor brought loads of students in to see her because she was a beautiful baby with a full head of auburn and gold hair and deep blue eyes. She was a very dainty child, very slight in stature. She was a very good child, extremely respectful to both herself and anyone she came into contact with. She was an excellent pupil in junior school and high school. She took a course in child development, typing and English and she passed them all.

Penny's parents split up when she was 13 and her brother was 11. Her father drank far too much and was violent towards her mother. He was never violent towards the kids, in fact Penny was a real daddy's girl, his princess. Alex was a mummy's boy, neither of them were any bother at this stage.

She started going out with her mother's friend's son at the age of 13. He has a serious drug habit 16 years on. The relationship fizzled out and at the age of 16 she met Brian. He was 23. When Penny was 18 she was given a one bedroom council flat in Hampstead. Brian moved in with her and life was great. Brian was working for his dad and Penny worked at the lido swimming pool in Hampstead and she loved it. At the age of 20 she found out that Brian was on heroin. She knew that he liked a joint and she didn't mind that. When he started going from bad to worse she asked the council if they would move her out of London so that she could get away from Brian. She was very anti-drugs at this stage. They moved her to Hoddeston. It was a lovely flat in a lovely area in Hertfordshire. Penny got a job at a solicitors in Temple. She would travel to London at 6.30am and get home at 8pm at night. After about 18 months she got very lonely and moved back to London. It was 1992 and her mother had to go into hospital for a triple by-pass. Penny was given a studio flat in Hampstead.

She was happy back in London with a good job and an excellent social life in top clubs like Browns and Stringfellows. She also had some excellent relationships, three TV actors and a doctor who she took home to meet the family. Her mother describes her as the perfect daughter at that time—trustworthy, attractive, smart, clean and kind. She had a great relationship with her brother Alex.

In 1994 her mother re-married. Alex became a father to Ashleigh in December 1994. her mother contacted her to tell her that she was an auntie and Penny spent seven hours with her family. A wonderful family time. Her nephew Adam was born in 1996 and yet again Penny was there at the hospital at 6am in the morning. She idolised those kids—she'd take them swimming, to the park, and to the fair.

In 1998 at the age of 28 Penny met a reformed drug addict. He'd been clean for seven years. At this time she truly believed him and this is where the story changes. She tried it three times and she was hooked. She won't go back to her flat because the dealers would be too far away and she couldn't bear it.

From then on she went down fast. By the end of 1999, her mother noticed how thin she'd got. When she asked her about it, she said that she'd been stressed out breaking up with her boyfriend. The boyfriend in question has since died. He laid in the gutter for five hours and passers by thought he was asleep. A friend told her mother the truth and when she confronted her she admitted the truth and said it was not a problem. I will now use the words her mother used to explain what life is like now.

"Well that was it really Georgie, since then she's gone from a beautiful young woman to someone I don't even know. From someone who used to shower twice a day to someone who hasn't had a bath in a year. She doesn't have hardly any teeth because someone broke her jaw in two places. The bone is infected and needs attention, but she refused to go for any treatment. When her jaw was broken she was clipping to get money for drugs. She's had septicaemia three times. I went to visit her in hospital. I was on the bus going home and she was stood there with the drip and all its attachments still in place in a pair of pussycat pyjamas. Everyone was staring but she didn't care. She couldn't stand it without her gear and walked out. She sleeps in doorways and bin cupboards or under the bridge on the canal. I live just above it knowing that she is there. Her father, who is both a drug addict and alcoholic, uses crack cocaine with his own daughter. She steals clothes from charity shops to wear or to sell and the worst part of all is that she is covered in open sores that ooze green puss and blood. Her beautiful red hair is filthy and matted, but she doesn't see herself like this. Her insight disappeared when she started using crack cocaine.

A few weeks ago she came round and her feet were cut to ribbons. I asked her where her shoes were and she said that someone must have stolen them while she was asleep. Three or four times a day she screams abuse at me through my patio door. I've taken out a court order and had her arrested eight times. Nothing that I do works or makes any difference whatsoever. Apart from all of this she has stolen from me many many times, an £800 set of saucepans, my gold, phones, videos, even children's presents. She has taken the clothes out of my tumble dryer, jars of coffee, and packets of washing powder and even my electric toothbrush. Penny is someone that I no longer know or recognise and yet I know she's in there somewhere. I will never really stop fighting in the hope that one day we find her. She comes to me three or four times a day just for money, never to say "How are you mum?" I miss her so much, as she's leaving she shouts "Love you mum" It's the same with her Nan, she visits her every day too, It's so sad when you can't let your own child into your home, but I can't cope with the stealing, the abuse and the violence. The other day my granddaughter said "Nan, I'm scared of how aunty Penny looks now". I will never give up hope that one day I can welcome her back, the beautiful woman she was and say "Penny, you're back, I've missed you so much". Penny's mother's words end with "that day will come, it has to"

Now to come to how I was able to relay this tragic story to you and probably the worst part of all. You know that case history No 1 is Emma (not her real name). This happens to be Penny's real name and as her mother is so devastated by all this she has allowed me to explain that she suggested I use the name Penelope Pittstop. She can't use this when she's arrested now because she's far too well known to the police. Last weekend Emma, who as you know is in rehab brought a young man to see me. His name is Alex and she met him in rehab. She had already sent me a letter Alex had written to his own addiction. They are told to do this whilst in rehab as part of their therapy. You will read his letter next. While he was talking to me, he told me about his sister and how his mother was at her wits end with a son in rehab and a daughter who is on death's door. As you can now see Alex is Penny's younger brother, unbelievable but true. When I explained that his sister's story would be a very powerful one he gave me his mother's telephone number and I rang her. At that time I had no idea what her reaction would be. It's hard to find the right words to say "Can I use your daughter as a case history for a book that I'm writing?" but I needn't have been worried because she not only agreed but also said "write about Alex too". As you can see she has supplied me with all the details and family photos, four of which clearly show the tragic decline in her lovely daughter during the five year duration of her addiction.

Following this chapter is her brother's letter in which he explains his anger and lots more. These are the photo's that say it all and if these don't put people off then I fear that nothing will. Her mother says that she can't believe it, one addict is bad enough but she has two. I do think there's hope for Alex. He told me that before he got into drugs he was earning really good money as a plumber and wants to go back to it. He wants his children to respect him and more then anything he wants to do it for his mum's sake. I pray to God that he will.

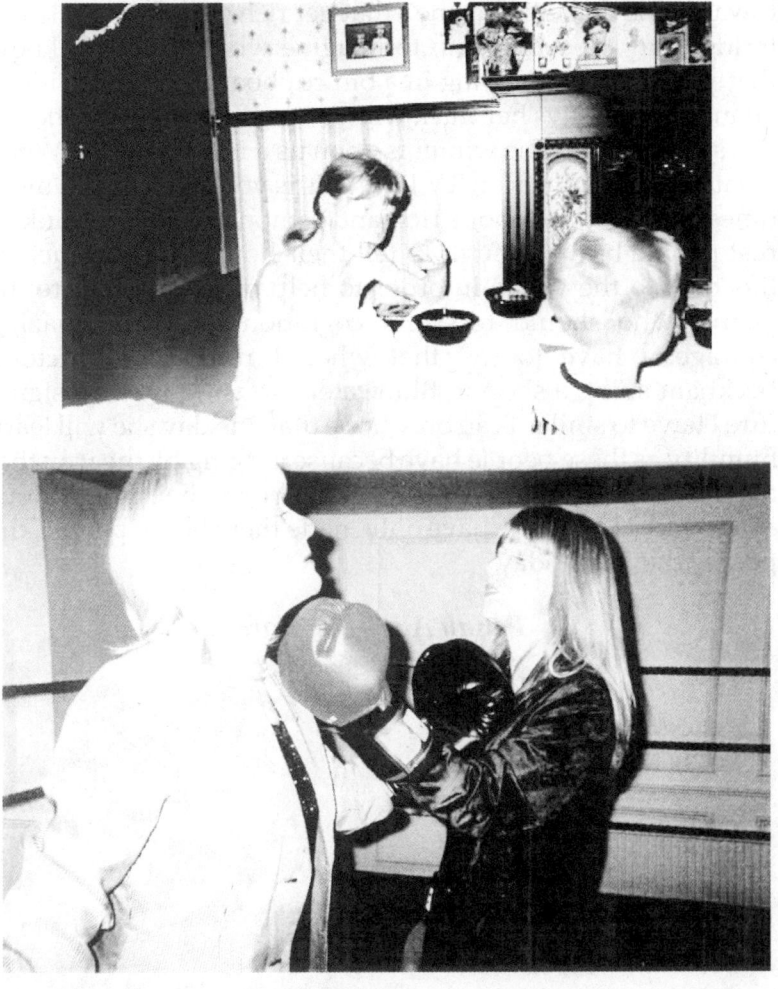

They Cut and Mothers Bleed

I felt I must write a tribute to the people who have helped me with this book and I have to say, most of all the mothers. They have been so strong and determined to help. Their attitudes are "if it will help others, we must tell our stories". There was no bitterness no "poor me" only a heart big enough to want to do anything they can to prevent young people ending up in the horrendous situation that their own kids are in. When I say no bitterness that's not strictly true. They are all bitter towards the dealers, the one's that get rich out of so much suffering. Can we even begin to imagine what it's like to know that your child is sleeping in a bin cupboard under a bridge? Penny's mum buys her thick winter coats from charity shops,. She says that now the winter is upon us it is even worse. When I watch programmes on TV like 'This is your life', which more times than not are about rich and famous people, I think of real people brave enough to tell their horror stories, such as this one, to the world in order to help others. These are the people who should receive recognition for their amazing courage. I have to say that when I read about Victoria Beckham suing a shop in Bluewater for using David's signature I have to smile. I can only hope that one day she will learn humility as these people have because judging by the way that they are so willing to help others, it shows their horrendous experiences in this life have only made them better people, the people they are today.

Penny Ain't No More

Long red hair with golden lights
A figure some would die for
Penny was a beauty
But Penny ain't no more

Her body's wrecked and broken
Someone broke her jaw
Penny once turned many heads
But Penny don't no more

She winces at the pain
From another open sore
Penny loved designer clothes
But Penny don't no more

She dosses down with winos
On a stone cold rock hard floor
She once lived in Hampstead Heath
But Penny don't no more

Her mother's cried a million tears
Her eyes are red and sore
She once had so many hopes
But her mother don't no more

Her ears are ever listening
For that knock upon the door
She dreads four words especially
Penny ain't no more

Addicts are told to write to the addict within them. This is Penny's brother's letter.

Letter To Addict

Addict listen up. You have taken enough from me. All you have ever given me is false hope. So this is where I tell you how I feel about you and why I need to go my own way. This has gone on for far too long—you have almost killed me and I can't take any more. I think back to when I was seven years old sitting at the back of the class. You made me think it was OK to sniff Tippex. I'd get so high and out of my head and then I'd black out. By the time I was eight, you showed me glue and told me not to tell anyone I was sniffing it. One day I walked through the flats sniffing it through a crisp packet, my mum caught me and called me over, but I didn't even recognise her. I felt so sad and ran away, but you convinced me that everything would be OK. I should have told you to go then, but I let you off the hook again. Several years later you convinced me that it was OK to smoke cannabis and sniff bottles of gas which I did for the next couple of years. I believed you when you told me that every thing was beautiful but not content with that you introduced me to ecstasy and LSD. I lost all of my teenage years and you stood back and watched it happen. I really believed that when I left school I would be capable of putting it all behind me and getting my life together again. Then you introduced me to cocaine, but I loved you for it. You advised me to inject it because the affects would fulfil me far more than sniffing it ever could. You allowed me to witness my sister killing herself. You said it was OK to run around the streets robbing together and then take scum drugs together. You made me scum, how could you let me forget my sister's needs and put drugs before her? Even when she was begging on the streets you didn't let me take care of her. I put you before my sister, how could you allow me to do that? Even though I loved her so much you let me watch while she wasted away to a bag of bones. Her body and her face have been ripped to pieces, I can never forgive you for letting me stand by and watch all of this taking place and to this day you've still got hold of my Emma, she's so vulnerable. She needs me to be in her life, but this time it has to be without you by my side. From now on I am putting my family first, you do not even come into the frame any more. You've took my life and my family's life. But that was yesterday, today I refuse to let you rule anymore. Why did you let me use crack at a funeral? How could you watch me lose everything? I was eating off of floors and sleeping in doorways. I felt so degraded. I abused it so much that I became convinced that I had living creatures under my skin. I was so paranoid I started to cut away at my own skin pulling bits of my own flesh out of me. How dare you do this to me? I just couldn't stop it, my own body will always remind me of you. I am scarred from head to toe. I was a ticking time bomb, I could have killed someone at any given moment. How I didn't take my own life is a miracle. I didn't have a single caring feeling inside of me, you turned me into an evil man and smashed my family to bits. I robbed, I stole and I manipulated everyone around me. You convinced me that drugs were more important than my loved ones. How could you let me turn my back on them? Not content with that you helped me to find a place in prison, you still couldn't leave me alone. You tried to convince me that it was the world's fault and that I'd be better off not living in it. You almost had me believing you, but God was on my side. He still is. You have taken so much from me. All I'm doing is putting pen to paper over a few pages, but as you know I would need thousands of pages to remind you of the heartache and pain that you have caused me. So much pain, a part of me wants to still be angry with you but I won't get those years back by being angry with you. Yes, you beat me, but that's the past. This is now and I'm starting my life again without you. I don't need you any more, I can't trust you, I will never let you fill me with that crap again. It kills me to think about what you put me through for one day let alone all those years. I want to be a good father to my children, I miss them so much and it wouldn't work with you in my life. My mum deserves a better son. Don't think you can take my family away from me again.

I've got this feeling of contentment and I'm really enjoying it. Realization is the word for me today. Recovery is making me feel content, everything is hitting home. I've just got to say no to picking up. All we talk about is recovery, I'm looking forward to tomorrow, I'm feeling really tired now so I'll say "Thank you Hope House and goodnight"

I deserve better, no more you and me, leave me alone, forget about me. I'm looking towards my goals and they don't include you. I need to move on and put you behind me. I need my life back and I'm taking it. I'll fight you to the death. I need love around me, my family are still here for me and I'm lucky to have them. As long as you keep out of my life, they will be here for me. you're on your own, it's over, finished. I'm much happier without you.

Alex Anderson

Hope

Without it there's no future
No comfort for the soul
We lose sight of life's pleasures
Without it there's no goal
Without it life seems pointless
With no respite for our pain
Our well-laid plans just crumble
Leaving nothing left to gain
It provides life's rhyme and reason
Our will to carry on
Our spirits lift regardless
It helps to keep us strong
Don't allow cruel fate to steal it
This friend who'll help you cope
It's yours and mine to treasure
So don't lose sight of hope

I asked Alex what he thought was the most important thing to remember and he replied "Hope"

7

A Few One Offs: A Final Summing Up and The Beginning

My Message to Addicts

These are just a few short stories that have been relayed to me by addicts who have known these people. One is about a barrister's son another about a girl who gave birth to a tiny baby addicted to heroin. The others are from my own thoughts

Heroin

Hero-in disguise
You're a hero if you use it
Many end up dead
Many will abuse it
Hero-in a spin
Going round the bend
Hero-in the vein
Shattered lives that will not mend
Hero-in the gutter
Syringe still in his arm
Was he born to be an addict
Did he mean to cause this harm?
Hero-in the ground
Wish he'd not been born
Heroin causes heartache
Family left to mourn

One Off—Passed from an addict

Harry – Nickname "H": Father – Barrister

This Hell

"I deal with losers like you every day of my life
I'm ashamed to say you're my son, to say it cuts like a knife
I sentence garbage like you, it's my job to send them down"
Self righteous, hardhearted bastard
Standing there in your cap and gown

"I despise junkies like you, with your selfish pathetic excuses
You've shamed your entire family, now everyone knows what the truth is
My son, the arrogant junkie, just look at the state of your mother
What a wonderful shining example, you are for your younger brother.

Sat here with my head in my hands in a dingy 8x8 cell
Though I detest him for screaming the truth
Drugs have dragged me down to this hell

Past Mistakes

He begs, he steals, he sells himself, he needs his bread and butter
A few soiled clothes, a sleeping bag; his home is in the gutter
But look closely at the man within, look deeply into his eyes
Look beneath his bleak appearance, he wears a good disguise

Five years ago a stockbroker, a house in Primrose Hill
Progressing swiftly on from cannabis, the next step was a pill
Look deeply beyond a sad neglect to a decent man within
He'll pay each day for past mistakes, the biggest? Heroin

A Final Summing up and Some Useful Information

Drugs are Such a Sin

Let's go on a trip, we can take my Mitsubishi
You can wear my Rolex, do you wanna try a mushie?
We can drive at a high speed
Young Charlie's coming too
Don't be a dope and chicken out
'C' sticks to me like glue
I swear you'll be in ecstasy
The weather forecasts snow
We'll buy some coke, roll on the grass
The weeds won't hurt us though
Coz I'm a silly scag head
And you're my heroin
What a whiz what a crack
Drugs are such a sin

Passing The Caviar

I've told her I don't want her body, I only want the dosh
You know the one I'm talking about, everyone calls her posh
They say she was pretty, a bit like Madonna, many moons ago
For me she'd need a paper bag, do you think I should give her a go?
No it's no good I need the money, I just ordered a brand new car
Convertible BM, just wait til you see it, would you pass the caviar?

Addicts language

No

Shall I, shan't I? will I? won't I?
Sample cannabis
Is it worth it? Is a smoke essential
To my futures list?

Do I need it? How will I feed it?
Eats up all your dough
I've made my mind up, my mates' life's fucked
No, No, No, No, No!!!!!

Shall I? Shan't I? Will I Wont' I?
Sample one small joint?
Is it worth it? Do I need it?
What would be the point?

Makes you mellow, makes you moody
Increases paranoia
Shuts down lives, ruins futures
No one would employ ya'

Can you blame them, when you've shamed them?
Families fall apart
Mate's wife left him, took the kids
Says it breaks her heart

No, you smoke it, I don't need it
Mate gets up to go
Yes I'm sure mate, Christ, you're a state
No, No, No, No, No!!!!!

A Final Summing up and Some Useful Information

Heroin's Pull

H *for the hell it's put us through*
Evil *ways is where it will take you*
Remember *don't pick up the dice*
Or *it's you who'll pay heroin's price*
Its *first hit will catch your breath*
Now *you've sampled it*
Shake hands with death

Play *safe there is too much to lose*
Understand *all the pitfalls and choose*
Learn *from others and don't be a fool*
Live *your life avoid "heroin's pull"*

Eating Dirt

Eat dirt and the taste will be vile
Addicts eat dirt all the while
Till they finally reach their lowest point
It all started with their very first joint
Never realised their need would drag them right down to their knees

Devoured fast and swallowed up whole
It finally destroys your soul,
So remember this don't eat dirt
Or you will end up very hurt!!

The Top Of The Pile

The druggies we see every day each have a story to tell
They stick together like glue on their separate journeys to hell
Ecstasy, now there's a name for it, Jesus that's so profound
If you make up your mind to sample some, first book your plot in the ground
It can boil your blood, it can scramble your head and unless you're lucky you'll end up dead
They grub around to pay for it just like sewer rats
Lining the dealers pockets, big fat evil rich cats
Some even rob their own mothers to quell the craving inside
The families finally lose count of how many tears they've cried
Dirty disposed-of syringes lie broken on littered stairs
He sidles up to his dealer who's more than willing to sell him his wares
He roars off in his Jag whispering loser under his breath
Now and again he has a good laugh when he hears of a premature death
But our junkie is flying high with diamonds behind his eyes
Soars like a golden eagle 'til he reaches the clear blue skies
With a thud he hits the ground and it's back to reality
The tears start to sting his eyes, when will he ever be free?
And tomorrow, what of tomorrow? back to playing the same old game
He'll stare at his punctured arms then struggles to find a vein
So don't be tempted by drugs, value the life that you've got
Or you'll end up in the same boat, on top of a pile of rot.

A Final Summing up and Some Useful Information

Natalie – 20 years old – Still Using

All Thanks To You

"He's very small" the midwife said
"He fits the palm of my hand
Mother's an addict, anonymous dad
Poor little mite wasn't planned"

"His breathing is rapid" the doctor said
"I don't like the look of his skin"
It was as if I was invisible
I knew I'd committed a sin

"Not much of a start" the midwife said
the doctor nodded his head
"My daughter's still trying" he muttered
"I wish he were her child instead"

"He'd have wanted for nothing" the midwife said
The doctor nodded once more
"Druggie scum – don't deserve him" she said
Backing out of the door

"My youngest addict" the doctor said
"I'm not sure this one will pull through"
"Did you hear what I said?" the doctor said
"And this is thanks to you"

Fancy Sharing

Junkies are all into sharing
You don't call a junkie a stinge
They share their booze share their gear
Some even share their syringe

They share each other's depravity
Some even share blood diseases
Hep B, Hep C – even AIDS
It's dirty, it's tragic, it's sleazy

Lets look at the whole sordid picture
On the surface they're kind and caring
In reality they'd bleed you dry
What do you think? Fancy sharing?

An Illness Or An Act Of Complete Selfishness?

And so like all things in life Addicts Language comes to an end. Time to reflect on what you've all learned from this book. I dare say you will all have conflicting views on the seven case histories and their reasons or excuses for taking drugs. One thing is certain, you don't have to be a rocket scientist to see that, although their backgrounds were very diverse (some were abused others were over-indulged), their stories all ended up in disaster. Like a derelict house on a windswept moor, drugs drag you down to your knees and my final comment is this. To put it bluntly, addicts do get some relief through their gear; their families and friends are the ones who suffer the most, which makes it an act of complete selfishness and the more they take the more selfish they all become. The craving for drugs becomes their sole reason for living and any emotional feelings disintegrate along with their lives.

    The further they sink in to the underworld that drugs create for them, the more pain their families go through. As Emma's mum says, "We are all in pain but we don't all stick a syringe in our veins. One thing I have learned by writing this book is that you can't generalise and no matter what reason people have for taking this path, they have to pay a very high price in the end.

Drugs have no preferences, no boundaries, there are no restrictions on whose life will be ruined, it matters not. Show me one person who has benefited from taking drugs! Meeting all of these people and witnessing their pain has been a very humbling experience. The stigma attached to drug addiction is similar to the stigma that we have experienced through schizophrenia and I am aware of the pain it causes. These people come from all walks of life and it's very unfair to brand them all as "low life scum". Similar to the words I read in the papers everyday describing people with schizophrenia "schizo, psycho, loony and nutter". We are all individuals and deserve to be treated as such and no matter what your thoughts are, look at the before and after photos of Penny and ask yourself if anyone would want to end up like this?

You are probably wondering what conclusions I have made. It is very difficult because although they are all doing the same thing and they are all hurting many other innocent people, their reasons do differ. At the end of the day, it is the families that suffer the most which is totally unfair. I do believe the government should take far harder lines when the dealers get caught—we are far too soft in this country which is why they do it and continue to get away with it. We could talk about it forever more, but it won't prove anything. Anna said the other day show me one person who has benefited from taking drugs. And that says it all.

A Final Message

And so, no matter what your thoughts are now, I'm sure we will all agree on one thing that for the families and friends of addicts, this has to be one of the most painful experiences that anyone has to go through. To watch someone who you love sinking into a life of depravity is beyond our comprehension and worsened by the fact that they inflict this life upon themselves. Whatever an addict's life was like before drugs are not the answer. I have written this final poem to try to help in some small way and, like the title of this book, it is a contradiction in terms. Although this is the end of the book, the title of the poem is "The Beginning", but it ends with the words, "the end". I do hope that this book goes someway, however small, to act as a deterrent to anyone contemplating making drugs a part of something as precious as "their life".

The Beginning

Life is very precious the start of each new day
You must search to find it's meanings
You must strive to find a way
Think of all the suffering endured by many more
Think of waves that break each day on each and every shore
Think about each sunset that paints each clear blue sky
Along with many pleasures enjoyed by you and I
Think about your loved ones who'd protect each breath you breathe
Think of how they'd suffer, think of how they'd grieve
Think about your mother's love so faithful to the end
She'll support you with her heart and soul, your ever-loving friend
Think about yourself now, free spirit and free soul
Think about your future make being clean your goal
Don't give in to drugs' temptations, the devil's evil friend
Think about the gift of life and don't let this be "The End"